PLACES FOR PLANTS

WHAT TO PLANT WHERE

JACQUELINE SPARROW

VIKING O'NEIL

Viking O'Neil
Penguin Books Australia Ltd
487 Maroondah Highway, PO Box 257
Ringwood, Victoria 3134, Australia
Penguin Books Ltd
Harmondsworth, Middlesex, England
Viking Penguin, A Division of Penguin Books USA Inc.
375 Hudson Street, New York, New York 10014, USA
Penguin Books Canada Limited
10 Alcorn Avenue, Toronto, Ontario, Canada M4V 1E4
Penguin Books (NZ) Ltd
182–190 Wairau Road, Auckland 10, New Zealand

First published by Penguin Books (NZ) Ltd, 1992

This edition published by Penguin Books Australia Ltd 1992

10 9 8 7 6 5 4 3 2 1

Chapter illustrations by Ann Skelly
Plant illustrations by Karen Walker
Designed by Suellen Allen

Printed and bound in Hong Kong

National Library of Australia
Cataloguing-in-Publication data

Sparrow, Jacqueline, 1930–
    Places for plants : what to plant where.

    Includes index.
    ISBN 0 670 90549 6

    1. Gardening. 2. Landscape gardening. I. Title.

635

CONTENTS

FOREWORD

The gardener's greatest dilemma is often what to plant where! In *Places for Plants*, Jacqui Sparrow offers us a refreshing approach to plant selection for many situations and many types of garden.

Jacqui is a widely respected New Zealand columnist and gardener who regularly spends time in Australia. Her knowledge of both Australian and New Zealand natives is extensive, and in this excellent book she covers a remarkably wide range of introduced as well as native plants.

Many of those common problem areas, such as plantings on banks and retaining walls, or along boundaries and entranceways, are discussed, with delightful suggestions for original planting combinations. Jacqui gives details of varieties and cultivars to suit every position, even covering colour plantings as well as details of propagation and care.

Places for Plants will enable us to plan an easy-to-establish garden which needs little maintenance, whatever its size or location, style or soil type. With the help of this handy reference we can choose plants to suit our local conditions, whether by the sea, in a shady corner, in a hot, dry area, or any other situation.

Symbols showing at a glance the light/shade preferences, height and flowering season of each particular plant are a bonus for the reader. They provide a quick, easy reference when choosing plants.

Readers will quickly find that Jacqui has a marvellous ability to simultaneously inform and entertain, her charming descriptions holding our interest throughout. She gives a fresh slant to species selection, and offers a wider variety of choice than many more conventional gardening books. I am very pleased to introduce *Places for Plants* to Australian gardeners.

Jane Edmanson, ABC-TV's *Gardening Australia*

KEY TO SYMBOLS IN PLANT LISTS

○   Full sun. The sunniest possible aspect is required for the plant.

◐   Partial sun or shade. The plant requires some sun but will do quite well in partial shade.

●   Full shade. The plant does well in a shaded position.

▲   Height. The figures given are an indication of the eventual height of the plant.

❖   Flowering season. Where no information is given the plant either does not flower or its flowers are inconspicuous.

INTRODUCTION

This book was written with the idea of helping gardeners to find the right plant for the right place. I myself have spent hours wandering round the garden with a plant bought on impulse, trying to find the right place for it. I realised I had been going the wrong way about it, putting the cart before the horse. And I cannot be the only one.

Gardens are exciting places, always on the move. In the home, once we have furnished the house to our satisfaction it remains the same, but the garden is constantly changing and growing, never static — a constant source of interest.

First make a plan of your garden and existing structures, and decide its purpose. It helps to work to a theme. The connection between house and garden is a basic part of garden design, and the view of the garden from the main rooms of the house is important. Choose your plants to create shelter, privacy and adornment. The plantings embellish and decorate the fixed uncompromising architectural structures of the garden — living furniture.

The climate is important to consider: prevailing wind directions, temperature extremes, soil and aspect. Always look at gardens in your area and note plants doing well there. Your aim should be an easy-to-establish, low-maintenance garden.

I must stress the importance of using botanical names wherever possible. It is a question of identity. The botanical name applies to only one plant, and is used internationally for instant recognition. The botanical name shows relationships between plants and families. Common names can be confusing, and wherever possible I have used them just as a guide.

I have endeavoured to show at a glance, by the use of symbols, the light preferences of plants, then the height, and this has been a concern. A tree or shrub may grow large and buxom in the perfect climate, and struggle elsewhere, so the heights given should be taken as a general guide only. And this is applicable for time of flowering, too. In mild winters, for instance, spring-flowering shrubs often surprise us with early bloom.

Success comes from choosing the right plant for the right place — understanding your situation and providing the best possible plant for your environment and purpose. I have tried to describe the most favourable conditions for plants in the average garden, and to stimulate interest in their use.

Mainly, and most importantly, gardens are fun. Places for enjoyment and for relaxation; the right place to refresh and revive flagging spirits. Good luck in yours.

Jacqueline Sparrow

BANKS AND RETAINING WALLS

1

Shrubs for banks • Climbers for banks • Perennials for banks • Annuals for banks • RETAINING WALLS • Shrubs for retaining walls • Climbers for retaining walls • Perennials for retaining walls

Banks are a part of many gardens, awkward unless planted with subjects to beautify and perhaps to prevent erosion. Banks can then become some of the prettiest garden features, giving dramatic impact. A host of plants is available for banks, sunny or shaded. These need to be able to survive the dry conditions often encountered on slopes.

Gentle slopes are easy to maintain. Steep banks will probably need draining and stabilising before planting. A bank may be so steep that a retaining wall becomes necessary. Many of the plants recommended for banks are just as suitable for retaining walls, from groundcovers and climbers to succulents and alpines.

Shrubs for banks

Shrubs for banks should be tough, hardy varieties, easily and quickly grown; shrubs which do not require fussing over. Species suitable for banks want a good root system to enable them to anchor firmly on their sloping site, and should be evergreen, ground covering and mound forming for preference.

CISTUS	◯
Rock Rose	▲50 cm–1.5 m
Cistaceae	❖ Spring–summer

Excellent shrubs for banks are the smaller, hill-hugging cistus. *Cistus* 'Sunset' has golden centres and flat single white flowers which are quite beguiling. Of course the rock rose also comes in pink and mauve, but the white variety is superior. *C. ladaniferus* is white, splashed wine and is a larger shrub. Poor, dry banks suit all cistus very well, and you can propagate them from cuttings with no trouble or by seed sown in spring.

CONVOLVULUS	◯
Ipomoea	▲50 cm
Convolvulaceae	❖ Spring–autumn

Convolvulus puts terror in gardeners' hearts. Not *Convolvulus cneorum*, an evergreen shrub which never intrudes, and does not produce suckers. It is pretty all year, with silky, silver, glistening leaves and white, sometimes flushed pink, flowers. A warm slope completely covered with this ipomoea is most spectacular — when the sun catches the silver leaves the whole bank will light up. *C. cneorum* is an easy-going shrub, and can be simply propagated from cuttings.

COTONEASTER	◯
Rosaceae	▲Prostrate; to 50 cm
	❖ Summer

Prostrate-growing *Cotoneaster horizontalis* and *C. conspicuus* both have brilliant red berries in the winter. Both can deal with cold; after all, one is from Tibet, the other from the high mountains of China. Hardy cotoneasters, tolerant of most soils, are the perfect choice for a difficult bank.

EURYOPS	◯
Compositae	▲to 2 m
	❖ All year, mostly winter

Bright yellow daisies cover *Euryops pectinatus* nearly all year long, coming to their best in winter just when you need them most. No trouble to grow, these daisies have no bad habits and are easily propagated — simply take cuttings when you feel like it. Also worthwhile are E. *athanasiae*, and E. *acraeus*, which is a smaller shrub. All have attractive grey-green foliage and prefer light, well-drained soil, although they will do very well on a clay bank.

GREVILLEA	○
Proteaceae	▲Prostrate; to 1 m
	❖ All year

Grevilleas are versatile Australian shrubs which thrive in difficult growing conditions. The flowers are delightful and come in warm colours, both soft and clear. Grevilleas hybridise very well and new varieties are appearing all the time. The foliage is invariably attractive, and the flowers encourage birds. New prostrate grevilleas are excellent bank plants, as are some of the small shrub types. *Grevillea* 'Robyn Gordon' is a fine, vigorous groundcover. G. *juniperina* thrives in light soil, but there are many to choose from.

JUNIPERUS	○◗●
Cupressaceae	▲Prostrate; to 50 cm

Some junipers spread, others are bolt upright — a versatile group. *Juniperus conferta*, of the spreading variety, is good for covering banks. It has pretty light-green foliage. J. *horizontalis* has glaucous green leaves and hugs the slope. Many more conifers are available. They are best grown with other plants, for a bank of only junipers could be rather dull.

OTHER SHRUBS SUITABLE FOR GROWING ON BANKS

Cytisus x *beanii* — broom
Eriostemon myoporoides — waxflower
Felicia angustifolia
Genista lydia — broom
Hebe
Hypericum — St John's wort
Lantana montevidensis

Leucospermum prostratum
Podalyria sericea — satin bush
Potentilla cultivars — cinquefoil
Protea
Pyracantha — fire thorn
Rosa — shrub types
Selago thunbergii

Climbers for banks

Climbers are an essential part of all gardens, and there is no need to resist a climber for a bank. A variety that digs its toes in and helps counteract erosion is the one to look for. Living on a bank is not always easy, and climbers need to be quick growing, vigorous and evergreen to cope with the conditions.

FICUS	○◐●
Creeping fig	▲To 10 m
Moraceae	

The creeping fig, *Ficus pumila*, is rather slow to take off, but when it does, look out. It attaches itself relentlessly to anything it comes across and takes steep banks entirely in its stride. The leaves of *F. pumila* grow small and dainty for a start, but get coarser as the vine ages. The cultivar 'Minima' can be more easily dominated. Soils of all types will suit this rampant climber.

HEDERA	○◐●
Ivy	▲3–6 m
Araliaceae	

Ivy has a place in so many areas of the garden and is excellent on a steep bank. English ivy, *Hedera helix*, is always pretty. *H. canariensis* has large, heart-shaped, glossy leaves. One form, 'Tricolor', has small silver-variegated leaves. Both species are easily propagated from rooted cuttings taken at any time. Admirable for erosion control, ivy makes few demands, but it does harbour slugs and snails. Watch where it goes; it can get out of hand. And do grow the hybrids. 'Goldheart' is just that, bordered green, golden-hearted.

LONICERA	○◐
Honeysuckle	▲To 10 m
Caprifoliaceae	❖Winter–spring

Evergreen *Lonicera japonica* is a rampant climber but does a great job of covering banks, even embankments. It needs to be watched — turn your back and it will naturalise. It is probably best to choose a less vigorous cultivar. *L. japonica* 'Aureo-reticulata' is a good variegated honeysuckle. Try some of the hybrids. Varieties of *L. periclymenum*, 'Belgica' and 'Serotina' are both sweet smelling, the flowers deep red in bud, opening to cream.

PANDOREA	○
Wonga wonga vine	▲To 6 m
Bignoniaceae	❖Spring–summer

The vigorous wonga wonga vine, *Pandorea pandorana*, has glossy foliage and white or cream-spotted flowers and will cover a bank, even a big one. It will grow in a wide range of climates and soils. This hardy Australian is not as choice as *P. jasminoides* but it is tougher.

ROSA	◯◗
Rose	▲To 10 m
Rosaceae	❖ Spring–autumn

The Macartney rose, *Rosa bracteata*, is used to combat soil erosion in some countries. This rose has bright, evergreen leaves and flowers of pure white with fluffy golden stamens. The creamy-primrose 'Mermaid' is one of its offspring. The Cherokee rose, *R. laevigata*, has enchanting single white flowers blooming very early in spring, with a later flowering in autumn. It is used in the United States to stop erosion on river-banks. Evergreen *R. wichuraiana* is excellent on banks, even shady slopes. It has single white flowers. Many hybrids from this rambler are available: 'Albertine', 'Albéric Barbier', 'Dorothy Perkins'.

OTHER CLIMBERS SUITABLE FOR GROWING ON BANKS

Bougainvillea
Hardenbergia — false sarsaparilla
Hibbertia scandens — guinea gold vine
Jasminum
Kennedia — coral pea

Solandra — cup of gold; chalice vine
Thunbergia gregorii — golden glory creeper
Trachelospermum jasminoides — Chinese star jasmine

Perennials for banks

AGAPANTHUS	◯◗
Amaryllidaceae	▲25 cm–1.5 m
	❖ Summer

For a large bank, hot and dry or damp and shady, the amazing *Agapanthus praecox orientalis* will grow wherever it is put. The blue or white flowers are perfect comple-ments for one another. Do grow them together, and admire them tumbling down a big bank. Always green, always attractive, these agapanthus deserve a place in every garden. Daintier deciduous varieties include *A. campanulatus* with soft to deep blue flowers, and *A. patens* which boasts a dark blue stripe down the centre of each light blue petal. *A. inapertus* is also deciduous, but larger, with long, stiff stems of dark blue to purple flowers. Agapanthus are simplicity itself to grow and seed so profusely they appear to reproduce by magic. They are easily increased by division.

GAZANIA	◯
Treasure flower	▲50 cm
Compositae	❖ Year round

Give them well-drained but poor soil in a sunny situation and South African gazanias will romp away. The gazanias we grow are mostly hybrids and they come in rich, dazzling colours almost too bright for some gardens. At the beach they are splendid; salt winds will not faze them. If you want quick colour, an oriental carpet on your bank, gazanias are for you.

HELIANTHEMUM	○
Rock Rose	▲25 cm
Cistaceae	❖ Spring–summer

Hardy *Helianthemum nummularium* and its hybrids are small plants smothered in blooms of yellow, apricot, white, cerise or orange. On a bank they shine. Helianthemums are not affected by the cold, have evergreen foliage from green to silver, and are happy by the sea and in hot, dry zones — altogether an amenable perennial. You need several to make a show, and you can propagate these from tip cuttings.

HELICHRYSUM	○
Compositae	▲10 cm
	❖ Summer–autumn

Helichrysum argyrophyllum is a shiny, silvery carpet all year, and in late, late summer and autumn small yellow daisies cover the silver leaves. Everlasting, the flowers can be cut for drying. It is very useful for banks, and has no enemies. Any type of well-drained soil will suit. You need several plants to start with. Propagate from cuttings. *H. retortum* has shiny white flowers and likes similar conditions.

OSTEOSPERMUM	○
Compositae	▲25–60 cm
	❖ Year round

Jolly good on banks, *Osteospermum ecklonis* has glistening pure-white flowers with a charming deep-blue centre. *O. fruticosus* is similar in growth and has mauve flowers. Easily propagated from cuttings, osteospermums (formerly dimorpotheca) are no trouble to grow, though they tend to get untidy and woody and need clipping back. Virtually any well-drained soil suits them. The flowers have a long season. Look for 'Starry Eyes' — it has unusual furled petals.

POLYGONUM	○◗
Polygonaceae	▲To 20 cm
	❖ Summer–autumn

Ground-covering *Polygonum capitatum* grows with rapidity. It has trailing stems which root at the slightest provocation, even in poor soil. Very good for a steep bank,

P. capitatum has pretty soft red leaves, turning crimson in autumn. The flowers are small pink neat ovals. Propagate by division.

Annuals for banks

Annuals play a part in bank planting. They can be used as quick fillers until the permanent shrubs and perennials take over. You can use any sturdy annuals recommended for gardens in dry areas (see Chapter 8), and seaside gardens (Chapter 9), or the following two old favourites.

ESCHSCHOLZIA	○
California poppy	▲20–40 cm
Papaveraceae	❖ Spring–summer

This poppy, *Eschscholzia californica*, is a natural for warm banks as it comes from the Californian hills. New eschscholzias have a wide colour range; look for the seed in single colours, from silky white to almost purple. The fluted flowers with a texture of Thai silk are good for cutting. California poppies are excellent by the sea and in cottage gardens. They thrive in most soil types and are raised from seed with the greatest of ease. Sow where they are to flower.

TROPAEOLUM	○◗
Nasturtium	▲To 2 m
Tropaeolaceae	❖ Winter–spring

One of the most useful annuals, the common nasturtium, *Tropaeolum majus*, will trail, climb, or keep to itself. And the colours are outstanding — from richest cream through to deepest red, and all the autumn shades in between. For a bank choose a trailing type from the new selected forms which have a brilliant colour range, and blankets of bloom. In pots, hanging baskets, in the cottage garden, versatile naturtiums provide a valuable service to the gardener. And you can eat them. The leaves and flowers are scrumptious in salads and the seeds make an acceptable caper substitute. 'Alaska' has variegated foliage.

RETAINING WALLS

Retaining walls are designed to stabilise steep areas, otherwise they would not be there at all. The building of such walls, often quite high, requires expertise. They can be made of interesting materials — rock, concrete blocks, wood or bricks. When they are dressed overall with plants, retaining walls can become some of the most presentable parts of the garden, using plants from groundcovers to climbers. Succulents are paragons for growing in crevices or rock walls, as are many alpines. Here is a selection of useful plants for spilling and trailing over retaining walls.

Shrubs for retaining walls

Shrubs suitable for growing on top of a retaining wall are those that satisfactorily droop and arch and have a strong root system. Undemanding shrubs, hardy and placid, with pleasant foliage and flowers, are the ones to choose.

CLIANTHUS	◯◗
New Zealand glory pea	▲ 1.5–3.5 m
Leguminosae	❖ Spring

An attractive New Zealand native, *Clianthus puniceus*, with its ferny foliage and rosy-red clusters of clawlike flowers, hangs over walls most agreeably. Slugs and snails will decimate the plant and even kill it, so watch out for them. *C. puniceus* will do well in any well-drained soil, and is easily propagated from seed or cuttings, best taken in autumn. Grow the ravishing white form too.

New Zealand glory pea

ERICA ○

Ericaceae ▲Prostrate; to 45 cm

❖ Winter–spring

If your area is suitable for ericas, give them a go. They come from two differing localities; the Europeans are hardy, but the South Africans appreciate more warmth. Hardy *Erica carnea* looks well on a wall. This is one of the prostrate ericas. *E. ciliaris* is also trailing, cold hardy and has réd flowers. All ericas must have lime-free soil. Add peat to the planting area, and make sure it is well-drained. Propagate from cuttings.

PLUMBAGO ○

Plumbaginaceae ▲4 m

❖ Summer–autumn

Plumbago auriculata (syn. *P. capensis*) has pale china-blue flowers, and grows quickly and strongly. It tumbles over a wall obligingly, spreading its beauty, or can be persuaded to climb upwards with equal ease. Plumbago blooms for many months and looks well in combination with white, deeper blue and lemon flowers. The white form of plumbago is just as vigorous. Any soil seems to suit plumbagos, but they will not tolerate frost.

ROSMARINUS ○◐

Rosemary ▲Trails to 2 m

Labiatae ❖ Spring–summer

Hardy rosemary, with aromatic leaves delicious in cooking, is good to grow. Poor soil and excessive heat do not worry this herb. *Rosmarinus* 'Prostratus' spills perfectly over walls; if you are going to grow just a single shrub over a wall, this could be the one. 'Blue Lagoon' is another rosemary for the same site. Its flowers are intensely blue. Rosemary is propagated from cuttings taken in autumn or winter.

OTHER SHRUBS SUITABLE FOR GROWING OVER RETAINING WALLS

Ceanothus — California lilac
Cotoneaster
Cytisus — broom (small species)
Daphne cneorum
Hebe
Jasminum nudiflorum

Juniperus horizontalis; J. sabina
Loropetalum — fringe flower
Rosa — bush varieties
Selago thunbergii
Streptosolen — marmalade bush

Climbers for retaining walls

Many of the climbers suggested for banks will happily cascade down a wall. Retaining wall climbers are those that will easily trail and spill.

HIBBERTIA ○

Guinea gold vine	▲To 3 m
Dilleniaceae	❖ Spring–summer

Tumbling over a warm wall, *Hibbertia scandens* is an arresting sight with large, glossy, yellow-gold single flowers, rose-like. This attractive vine appreciates medium-to-rich soil, a summer mulch, weekly watering and a nearly frost-free position.

JASMINUM ◯◗

Chinese jasmine	▲2–6 m
Oleaceae	❖ Winter–spring

Jasminum polyanthum curtains a wall with dainty pink buds opening to heavily scented ivory flowers. This jasmine comes from China, withstands frosts, and will grow in any well-drained soil. In some areas it has naturalised. After flowering, cut back *J. polyanthum* as it can become rampant.

PELARGONIUM ◯◗

Climbing geranium; ivy-leaved geranium	▲2–3 m
Geraniaceae	❖ Summer–autumn

Climbing geranium, *Pelargonium peltatum*, will climb up obligingly or hang decoratively. In shades from white to pink, mauve, red, and also bi-coloured, pelargonium varieties are handsome, hardy and evergreen, and grow so easily from cuttings. Their only vice is that they get woody, but after a pruning back, off they go again.

OTHER CLIMBERS SUITABLE FOR GROWING OVER RETAINING WALLS

Ficus pumila — creeping fig
Hardenbergia — false sarsaparilla
Hedera — ivy
Kennedia — coral pea
Lonicera — honeysuckle
Rosa — climbing and rambling types
Thunbergia alata — black-eyed Susan
Trachelospermum jasminoides — Chinese star jasmine

Perennials for retaining walls

Apart from sempervivums and other crevice plants often used in rock gardens, trailing and creeping perennials to spill over walls are the logical choice.

AUBRIETA ○

Cruciferae	▲Trails to 25 cm
	❖ Spring–summer

Aubrieta deltoidea is a pretty plant, mat-forming and at its best on walls. It has numerous hybrids, all in pink to purple shades. The blooms cover the plant, and it is best to cut aubrieta back hard after flowering. Not suitable for the seaside or humid areas, these plants enjoy cold conditions and any well-drained soil with lime. You can propagate them from seed, but they are variable. Arabis and aubrieta grown together are most pleasing.

CERASTIUM	○
Snow-in-summer	▲Trails to 1 m
Caryophyllaceae	❖ Spring–summer

On sunny walls *Cerastium tomentosum* is most satisfying, with glistening white flowers starring its silvery leaves for many months. Snow-in-summer is enchanting when grown with *Convolvulus mauritanicus* in this situation, or less vertical positions, in any well-drained soil.

CONVOLVULUS	○◗
Convolvulaceae	▲Trails to 2 m
	❖ Spring–autumn

Convolvulus mauritanicus has charming lavender-blue flowers lasting for many months, and the leaves are grey-green, dainty and attractive. This convolvulus tumbles prettily over a wall and is easily kept under control. It prefers warm conditions, well-drained soil and is propagated from cuttings. *C. cneorum*, ideal on banks, is also most useful on walls.

HELICHRYSUM	○
Compositae	▲Trails to 1.5 m
	❖ Spring

Helichrysum petiolatum 'Limelight' glows as it tumbles down a wall. The species is also pretty, with grey leaves. Both are ornamental all year round, and are grown for the foliage; the insignificant flowers make no impression. Cut these plants back occasionally, for they get straggly. They are propagated from cuttings taken at any time it seems. *H. argyrophyllum* is good for walls too.

OTHER PERENNIALS SUITABLE FOR GROWING OVER RETAINING WALLS

Arabis — rock cress
Aurinia saxatilis (syn. *Alyssum saxatile*)
Campanula isophylla — bellflower
Erigeron karvinskianus — babies' tears

Heterocentron elegans — Spanish shawl; heeria
Iberis sempervirens — candytuft
Lampranthus — ice plant
Lithodora diffusa 'Heavenly Blue'
Osteospermum

BEDS AND BORDERS

2

The idea of beds and borders has been constantly developing since Tudor times. At the end of the nineteenth century Gertrude Jekyll and William Robinson were responsible for designing borders with colour harmonies and texture. Traditionally borders were made up of herbaceous perennials. Miss Jekyll emphasised silver and grey plants, which have made such a comeback.

Today, beds and borders incorporate shrubs, perennials, annuals and bulbs, and are one of the most decorative elements in any garden, offering year-round colour and interest. Decide on your own garden requirements, and design your beds and borders in a style sympathetic to that of your house. Today's gardens go for a more relaxed, natural look, with plantings needing as little maintenance as possible. Consider harmonious colour schemes and obtain your effects with mass or repeat plantings of a few ideal varieties rather than single specimens of every shrub or plant that takes your fancy. Beds and borders should be a tapestry of felicitous colour.

SHRUBS FOR BEDS AND BORDERS

Look at the garden as a whole when selecting shrubs for beds and borders. Use shrubs which grow well in your area, and study their aspect and soil requirements. Smaller shrubs are best for beds and borders. They will have to compete with all your other border inhabitants, and you do not want the shrubs you select to take over and throw too much shade on other plants. Conifers and other ornamentals grown for foliage combine well with flowers. Do not forget shrub roses in all their glorious shades, but do choose varieties with your overall colour scheme in mind.

Shrubs with white flowers

HYDRANGEA	◯◑
Saxifragaceae	▲To 3.5 m
	❖ Early summer–autumn

Hydrangea paniculata 'Grandiflora' has pyramid-shaped panicles of white flowers fading to pink, and staying on the shrub for a long while, well into autumn. This is a showy deciduous shrub and does well with little fussing, but will respond to feeding, hard pruning and thinning. Other hydrangeas are white too. *H. arborescens* is lovely, and of course the popular *H. macrophylla* has some outstanding white varieties. *H. quercifolia* has white flowers. Hydrangeas like a moist soil and are easily propagated from cuttings.

SWAINSONA	◯◑
Leguminosae	▲1 m
	❖ Spring–summer

Swainsona galegifolia 'Albiflora' is a dainty shrub for the border, with paper-white pea-like flowers covering the bush on arching stems. Two or three plants together are best, underplanted with perennials. Frost-tender and requiring well-drained soil, swainsonas are not long lived.

VIBURNUM	◯◑
Caprifoliaceae	▲1.5–2.5 m
	❖ Early spring

Most viburnums are blessed with fragrance. *Viburnum* x *burkwoodii* has beautiful white flowers flushed pink in bud with a heady, spicy, haunting scent difficult to describe. *V. carlesii* is a more rounded and bushy shrub, but with flowers similar and a perfume just as sweet. These two are deciduous, as are most viburnums. They are excellent for borders and beds, especially near patios and decks. They tolerate cold, are hardy and not fussy over soil. You need to cut them back after flowering and you can propagate them from cuttings. *V. opulus* 'Sterile', the snowball tree, is a larger viburnum, more suitable for specimen plantings.

Shrubs with blue flowers

CEANOTHUS	○
Californian lilac	▲Prostrate; to 2.5 m
Rhamnaceae	❖ Spring–summer

Quick-growing, eye-catching shrubs, the ceanothus, with over 40 species, are all native to North America. In colours of intense blue, violet, purple and white, they look well in a mixed border. Many of the best are hybrids. Groundcovering *Ceanothus gloriosus* and C. 'Blue Gem' are excellent for dry conditions at the front of the border — grow several together. *C. papillosus* 'Roweanus' is a tall-growing shrub with cobalt-blue flowers. There are many others to choose from. Grow ceanothus in light, well-drained soil. Propagate them all from cuttings, and give them a mulch for the summer.

CERATOSTIGMA	◐
Chinese plumbago	▲80 cm–1 m
Plumbaginaceae	❖ Summer–autumn

Ceratostigma willmottianum has brilliant blue flowers on a small, twiggy bush. Deciduous in cool climates, it flowers for months on end, and is not at all fussy where it does so. Chinese plumbago looks best when grown in small groups amongst soft pastel-coloured flowers and lavenders, or under roses. It will self-seed, or you can grow it from cuttings.

CLERODENDRUM	○
Blue butterfly bush	▲1.5 m
Verbenaceae	❖ Summer–autumn

Smothered with clouds of two-toned velvety cobalt and sky-blue butterfly flowers, *Clerodendrum ugandense* is an enchanting sight. It is hardy so long as you give it well-drained soil, and it will grow at the coast if sheltered from strong winds. This shrub is most attractive when grown with silver-leaved artemisias, or flamboyant hibiscus and sky-blue-flowered *Plumbago auriculata*. Easily propagated from seed or cuttings, *C. ugandense* is truly a beauty.

OTHER SHRUBS WITH BLUE FLOWERS SUITABLE FOR BEDS AND BORDERS

Caryopteris x *clandonensis*
Felicia angustifolia
Hebe 'Blue Gem'
Hydrangea
Lavandula — lavender

Lechenaultia biloba
Olearia phlogopappa
Oxypetalum — tweedia
Plumbago auriculata
Rosmarinus — rosemary
Salvia mexicana

Shrubs with pink or red flowers

CANTUA	○
Magic flower of the Incas	▲2 m
Polemoniaceae	❖ Spring

It has to be admitted evergreen *Cantua buxifolia* can get long and straggly, but grow it for the magic of its multi-coloured blooms. This is a much neglected shrub and not grown as often as it should be. The flowers are tubular, rosy-red with yellow streaks, or pink and red. Prune after flowering. Any well-drained soil suits cantuas.

LAGERSTROEMIA	○
Crepe myrtle	▲40 cm–4 m
Lythraceae	❖ Summer–autumn

Deciduous *Lagerstroemia indica* and its hybrids are shrubs of great beauty, with crinkly blossoms smothering the bush for a month or more. A well-drained soil and a warm spot are essentials for success. Lagerstroemia will tolerate light frosts. Miniature cultivars are available for the smaller garden. Propagate the dwarf variety from mixed-colours seed. *L. indica nana* has carmine, rose, lilac and white shades, and the seeds germinate quickly and easily. With their rosy blossoms, lagerstroemias are very effective in summertime cottage gardens.

LUCULIA	○
Rubiaceae	▲1–2 m
	❖ Winter

Luculia gratissima is a most desirable shrub, filling the garden with its intoxicating perfume and pastel pink flowers when winter is at its worst. In cooler regions *L. gratissima* is often grown against a wall for frost protection but in warmer areas it does very well in the border as long as it is not crowded. Prune after flowering. It is a bit tricky to get cuttings to take — best to buy a plant.

THRYPTOMENE	○
Heath myrtle	▲1–2 m
Myrtaceae	❖ Winter–spring

Dainty Australian shrubs, with a delicious light fragrance and myriad tiny pink flowers on arching stems, *Thryptomene saxicola* and its cultivars are hardy, and extremely pretty in mixed beds and borders. Thryptomenes need a well-drained, light, almost sandy soil to do well. *T. calycina* has small white flowers, pink in the bud. Propagate from cuttings.

OTHER SHRUBS WITH PINK OR RED FLOWERS SUITABLE FOR BEDS AND BORDERS

Azalea — evergreen types
Boronia heterophylla, B. thujona
Coleonema — pink diosma
Crowea — waxflower
Daphne
Deutzia
Euphorbia pulcherrima —
   poinsettia
Grevillea
Hibiscus rosa-sinensis and hybrids,
   H. syriacus
Hydrangea
Kalmia — calico bush

Leptospermum — manuka; tea tree
Leucadendron 'Safari Sunset'
Paeonia suffruticosa — tree peony
Pimelea rosea
Podalyria sericea — satin bush
Prostanthera 'Rosea' — mint bush
Punica — pomegranate
Rhaphiolepis — Indian hawthorn
Rhododendron
Ribes — flowering currant
Spiraea japonica 'Anthony
   Waterer'

Shrubs with yellow and gold flowers

CHIMONANTHUS	○
Wintersweet	▲1 m
Calycanthaceae	❖ Winter

Wintersweet, *Chimonanthus praecox*, is grown mainly for its tantalising, seductive perfume. The lemon flowers are small and waxy, produced on leafless branches. Not a bit of good on its own, wintersweet needs companions in a bed or border. Easily grown, it will produce its perfumed flowers wherever you put it, as long as the position is moderately sunny and has well-drained soil. A branch of wintersweet in a room will send its fragrance through the house. Look for the larger-flowered variety.

POTENTILLA	○
Cinquefoil	▲Prostrate; to 1 m
Rosaceae	❖ Spring–autumn

Dear wee plants, not at all susceptible to cold and very easy to grow, shrubby potentillas are most successful in beds and borders. *Potentilla fruticosa* is yellow flowered, and has hybrids with grey-green foliage and with creamy-lemon blooms. Propagate by cuttings.

STREPTOSOLEN	○
Marmalade bush	▲1.5 m
Solanaceae	❖ Spring–summer

Orange and lemon flowers cover the rather lax, bushy *Streptosolen jamesonii* for many months. In cold areas the marmalade bush will be better in a pot in a conservatory as long as it can be taken outdoors every now and again. In warm gardens *S. jamesonii* is pretty amongst other shrubs, and looks well next to one of the yellow or red New Zealand flaxes, *Phormium tenax* hybrids. It will grow well over a wall. This bush will not tolerate frost, but stands up to salty winds at the beach. Propagate from tip cuttings.

OTHER SHRUBS WITH YELLOW AND GOLD FLOWERS SUITABLE FOR BEDS AND BORDERS

Azalea Mollis
Boronia megastigma
Cytisus — broom
Edgeworthia — yellow daphne
Forsythia
Grevillea
Halimium

Hibiscus rosa-sinensis and hybrids
Hypericum — St. John's wort
Kerria
Lantana hybrids
Leucadendron floridum,
   L. laureolum
Leucospermum

PERENNIALS FOR BEDS AND BORDERS

Perennials are the mainstay of beds and borders. Hardy herbaceous perennials are those which die down after flowering each year — the perennials native to cold climates. Evergreen perennials are just that, only the flowering stems fading, leaving leaves intact. Aim for succession and continuity of bloom, plan colour schemes as well as selecting for textures, and be aware of the height of plants in relation to annuals and shrubs you will be planting your perennials amongst.

If you dead head your plants regularly, you will ensure a long flowering season. Remove spent flowers with shears to promote bloom.

The choice of perennials is overwhelming, and here they are listed by individual colours. Do not forget perennials grown for foliage, such as New Zealand flax and large-leaved hostas, for instance. And grow silver-leaved plants which are such a foil for bright companions (see p.33).

Perennials with white flowers

ARABIS	○
Rock cress	▲To 20 cm
Cruciferae	❖ Spring

Arabis albida 'Flore Pleno' is a double snow-white arabis which looks extremely effective as an edging. This variety is much favoured for borders in the parks and large estate gardens of the Southern Highlands of NSW. Milton Park and Moidart, two of Australia's finest gardens, employ it extensively as an edging. Arabis has grey-green leaves and does well in cool climates.

GYPSOPHILA	○
Caryophyllaceae	▲To 1 m
	❖ Summer

Gypsophila paniculata and the cultivar 'Bristol Fairy' are enchanting in a mixed border. With airy, ethereal clouds of double white flowers, 'Bristol Fairy' is an asset to any garden. Well-drained soil, lime enriched, is what gypsophilas like. And they are one of the most useful flowers for cutting. They dry with great ease and stay pretty for years. Not easy to propagate, but plants last for a good many years once established. There are annual kinds too.

MALVA	○
Mallow	▲60–90 cm
Malvaceae	❖ Summer–late autumn

Musk mallow, *Malva moschata* 'Alba', is whiter than white, and very hardy and adaptable in the border. M. *moschata* has satiny flowers with a smell of musk. It self-seeds with abandon, which is just as well as it is short lived. Do not give mallows too rich a soil, and watch out for rust.

OTHER PERENNIALS WITH WHITE FLOWERS SUITABLE FOR BEDS AND BORDERS

Achillea 'The Pearl'
Anemone — Japanese
Aquilegia — columbine
Campanula — bellflower
Cerastium — snow-in-summer
Chrysanthemum — florists;
   marguerite; shasta daisy
Convallaria — lily-of-the-valley
Crambe cordifolia
Dianthus — carnation, pink
Gaura lindheimeri

Iberis — candytuft
Impatiens — busy Lizzie
Iris — bearded
Liatrus spicata var 'Alba' —
   blazing star
Paeonia — peony
Phlox
Polygonatum — Solomon's seal
Scabiosa — scabious; pincushion
   flower
Verbena

Perennials with blue flowers

CAMPANULA	◯◐
Bellflower	▲Prostrate; to 1.5 m
Campanulaceae	❖ Summer

Easy plants to grow, and in delightful shades of soft pink, blue and white, campanulas deserve a place in most gardens. These versatile plants come in sizes from groundcover to large spikes over a metre high. *Campanula isophylla* is low growing and dainty; *C. persicifolia* has large, delphinium-blue bells. *C. primulifolia* has dark violet flowers and grows to a metre high. There are a great many to choose from in delightful blues. It is easy to raise campanulas from seed. Great in the border with roses and shrubs, in fact a treasure anywhere in the garden.

DELPHINIUM	◯◐
Ranunculaceae	▲To 1.5 m
	❖ Summer

Delphinium x *belladonna* is a medium-sized delphinium and its cultivars have a wide variety of blue flowers with branching spires — ideal for beds and borders. Delphiniums are much hybridised and 'Pacific Giants' are deservedly popular. A smaller variety is available, 'Pacific Giants Dwarf Blue Spring'. Indispensable in the cottage garden and easily raised from seed, delphiniums fit in with most colour schemes.

ERYNGIUM	◯◐
Sea holly	▲To 1.2 m
Umbelliferae	❖ Summer–autumn

Eryngium giganteum has unusual prickly, metallic-blue flowers which dry perfectly. Some varieties are silvery-blue. *E. delaroux* loses its blue colour in winter and turns a vivid lime-green; *E. maritimum* is steel blue with splendid silvery bracts and enjoys a hot spot; *E. alpinum* is miniature. Sea hollies look well with other blue flowers, silver-leaved artemisias and pink flowers.

OTHER PERENNIALS WITH BLUE FLOWERS SUITABLE FOR BEDS AND BORDERS

Aster — Michaelmas daisy
Agapanthus
Aquilegia — columbine
Commelina coelestris
Echinops — globe thistle
Heliotropium — cherry pie; heliotrope
Iris — bearded

Linum — perennial flax
Meconopsis betonicifolia — Himalayan blue poppy
Omphalodes
Platycodon — balloon flower
Pulsatilla — pasque flower
Salvia

Perennials with pink or red flowers

ARMERIA	○
Thrift; sea pink	▲To 30 cm
Plumbaginaceae	❖ Spring–summer

Excellent for edging the border, sea pink *Armeria maritima* has rosy round flowers, and naturally does well by the sea. Thrift is tolerant of drought and tough conditions. Some of the hybrids have large, almost golfball-sized deep-pink blooms. These are good for cutting. Thrift is propagated by division or seed.

PAEONIA	○◐
Peony	▲70 cm
Paeoniaceae	❖ Spring

For borders in cool regions the beautiful, blowsy herbaceous hybrid peonies cannot be bettered. With attractive foliage, and good for cutting, the long-lived peony is a perfect perennial, associating well with many other plants, shrubs and bulbs. Peonies like a deep, cool, rich soil with good drainage and plenty of compost enriched with old animal manure. Do not disturb. Dozens of excellent hybrids exist, and many are pink and red. Peonies are ancient flowers, and still amongst the very best. Propagate by division and seed.

REHMANNIA	○
Chinese foxglove	▲To 1 m
Scrophulariaceae	❖ Summer

With bright pink foxglove-like flowers on tall, sturdy stems, *Rehmannia elata* is hardy in warm districts. It can be grown as a biennial and does very well in the mixed border. *R. elata* will grow from seed and flower in the first year; the plants tend to sucker. Grow it with artemisia, stachys and santolina.

OTHER PERENNIALS WITH PINK OR RED FLOWERS SUITABLE FOR BEDS AND BORDERS

Aster — Michaelmas daisy
Astilbe
Bergenia
Canna
Chrysanthemum coccineum — painted daisy; *C. frutescens* — marguerite; florist's chrysanthemum
Dahlia
Diascia

Gerbera
Helianthemum — rock rose
Hemerocallis — day lily
Impatiens — busy Lizzie
Lychnis — campion
Penstemon
Saponaria — soapwort
Sedum spectabile
Thalictrum — meadow rue
Verbena

Perennials with yellow and gold flowers

ALSTROEMERIA	◗
Peruvian lily	▲To 1 m
Alstroemeriaceae	❖ Spring–summer

Alstroemerias have been hybridised and improved greatly, mainly with the florist's trade in mind, as the flowers are so long lasting. *A. ligtu* hybrids are old favourites and well worth cultivating. In apricot, pink, red, orange and yellow tones, some with touches of green, hybrids are most handsome. Alstroemerias can be increased by division, but they prefer to be left undisturbed. They appreciate rich, moist but well-drained soils.

ANIGOZANTHOS	○
Kangaroo paw	▲To 2 m
Haemodoraceae	❖ Spring–summer

From Western Australia, kangaroo paws are splendid plants, and some are hardy in the border, needing no special attention. *Anigozanthos flavidus* and hybrids require very well-drained soil and sun, as do most subjects from WA. This species grows tall and complements many other perennials with its long stems of unusual flowers. Its soft lime colour is a good foil for blue flowers and stronger yellow blooms. There are many hybrids, some of them spectacular in their flamboyant colour combinations: yellow with red, yellow with orange, yellow with green and gold. *A. pulcherrimus* is a hardy yellow-flowering species. Kangaroo paws flower for six months at a time in warm areas, and the hardy species are tolerant of light frosts. Slugs and snails are partial to the young growths. Most kangaroo paws can be raised from seed, but nurseries supply plants of many of the cultivars.

HEMEROCALLIS	○◗
Day lily	▲30 cm–1 m
Liliaceae	❖ Nearly all year

Amongst the finest of perennials, day lilies are easy to grow and not troubled unduly by pests and diseases, although slugs and snails like the new leaves. Some varieties are dormant in cool areas. Day lilies are available in dozens of named varieties and it is best to obtain them from a specialist grower. They thrive in a wide range of soils and climates, and are most versatile. Day lilies look well with agapanthus and other bold flowers, under shrubs or in the border. They are so amenable you can grow them wherever you have space in the garden. The colours of the hybrids are exquisite — creamy-lemon, yellow, warm apricot and gold. Some are two-toned, and of course other brilliant colours are available.

Skilful use of plants and materials has produced impressive garden highlights to decorate banks and walls.

Here colour co-ordinated
borders employ both subtle and
dramatic schemes, and use is
made of contrasting shapes and
garden structures for added
impact.

Perennials with grey or silver leaves

CYNARA	◯
Cardoon; globe artichoke	▲1.5 m
Compositae	❖Summer

Bold, large-leaved cardoon, *Cynara cardunculus*, with its mauve thistle flowers is striking, forms a big clump and is very effective in the larger border. Globe artichoke, *C. scolymus*, is smaller and has the advantage of having a tight bud that is delectably edible. Ornamental architectural grey leaves, complete with the plump delicacy, make artichokes outstanding, and it should be grown far more than it is. Moreover, any buds you can bear to leave will turn into fluffy mauve flowers which dry well. Propagate by division or seeds.

FESTUCA	◯
Blue fescue	▲15–25 cm
Gramineae	

Blue fescue, *Festuca ovina glauca*, comes in handy for edging, on banks and anywhere you need a stalwart groundcover. It has quill-like leaves and contrasts well with flowering plants in beds and borders. *F. glacialis* has silvery leaves and is slightly smaller. Cut back these fescues ruthlessly and divide every year or so.

STACHYS	◯
Betony; lamb's ear	▲30–45 cm
Labiatae	❖ Summer

Stachys byzantina (syn. *S. lanata*) has large (15 cm) silver leaves which hug the ground. Its woolly, silvery-white foliage shows up well in any sunny situation. *S.* 'Limelight' has a lighter green foliage. Child's play to grow, stachys are tolerant of most well-drained soils and endure hot conditions. They are a great support in beds and borders, a touch of grey magic, and in moonlight and at dusk take on a luminous quality.

OTHER PERENNIALS WITH GREY OR SILVER LEAVES SUITABLE FOR BEDS AND BORDERS

Artemisia
Astelia chathamica
Centaurea clementii
Cerastium — snow-in-summer
Dianthus 'Mrs Sinkins' — pinks
Echinops — globe thistle

Helichrysum argyrophyllum
Hosta sieboldiana
Lychnis — campion
Salvia argentea
Sedum — stonecrop
Sempervivum — houseleek
Senecio cineraria — dusty miller

BULBS FOR BEDS AND BORDERS

Bulbs are a great asset to beds and borders, giving a fresh look at times of the year when many perennials and annuals are either dormant or not flowering. Of all the flowering species, bulbs probably give the most for the least effort, storing their goodness in their own packages. Bulbs are layers of fleshy leaf-scales containing a reserve supply of food. They are compatible with other bedding plants and are often combined with annual groundcovers for protection and effect. Many bulbs do not need lifting at the end of the season, although choice tulips, hyacinths and florists' gladioli benefit from drying off and storing. The small bulbs can be grown in pots and placed in beds and borders as they come into flower.

Bulbs with white flowers

CRINUM	○
Amaryllidaceae	▲1 m
	❖ Summer

Crinum powellii and its attractive hybrids have large bulbs and large flowers too, and are useful for awkward areas in beds and borders in larger gardens. Very easy to grow, crinums need a well-drained soil and a warm spot, frost free. Have the upper part of the bulb just immediately below the surface. Crinums enjoy a compost mulch. They look well growing with agapanthus and verbenas. You can propagate them from seed as well as from offsets.

GLADIOLUS	○
Iridaceae	▲50 cm
	❖ Early Summer–autumn

Hardy gladioli are excellent in beds and borders. The dainty *Gladiolus* x *colvillei* (sometimes listed as *nanus*) 'The Bride', pure white with an apple-green centre, is enchanting. Other hardy species have white flowers, e.g. G. *byzantinus*. You can leave the corms of these species in the ground — but the large-flowered florist's gladioli corms must be lifted. Hardy hybrids include 'Butterfly Hybrids' with ruffled flowers. Well-drained soil and a spot out of the wind suits them; staking is not necessary.

ZEPHYRANTHES	◐
Zephyr lily	▲25 cm
Amaryllidaceae	❖ Late summer–autumn

Grown in clumps at the edge of beds and borders, *Zephyranthes candida* from Argentina bears crocus-like white flowers at a time of year when beds and borders are looking tired. Easy to grow, *Z. candida* blooms freely and faithfully year after year and multiplies quickly, its clean flowers popping up where you least expect them.

OTHER BULBS WITH WHITE FLOWERS SUITABLE FOR BEDS AND BORDERS

Colchicum — autumn crocus
Crocus
Eucomis — pineapple flower
Freesia
Fritillaria meleagris
Galtonia — summer hyacinth
Hyacinthus
Iris — Dutch and English types

Lilium
Muscari azureum 'White Feather'
Narcissus
Nerine — spider lily
Ornithogalum — chincherinchee; star of Bethlehem
Tulipa
Watsonia — bugle lily

Bulbs with blue flowers

IRIS	○
Iridaceae	▲50–70 cm
	❖ Winter–spring

Iris are a large, beautiful family, some bulbous, others tuberous rhizomes. Amongst the bulbous are many with glorious blue blooms. The English, Dutch and Spanish iris (Xiphium group) are hardy species and hybrids. *Iris tingitana* has large, sky-blue flowers in winter. The Dutch hybrids look similar, although they are later to flower, and come in other colours, too — a rainbow of shades. A netted iris, *I. reticulata*, has purple flowers, but its hybrids contain many enchanting blues. Grown in drifts or amongst shrubs in the border, iris are superb.

MUSCARI	◐
Grape hyacinth	▲12–25 cm
Liliaceae	❖ Winter–late spring

Muscari are hardy, and grow beautifully in beds and borders, mainly as an edging. Usually blue, with grassy leaves, grape hyacinths come in many varieties and flower over a long period. It is easy to confuse them, as many look alike. One with a difference is M. *comosum plumosum*, with plumes of brilliant blue. Another worth watching for is M. *paradoxum*, the flowers of which are deepest royal blue, just about navy.

SCILLA	◯◗
Liliaceae	▲15 cm–1 m
	❖ Winter–spring

Despite its name, *Scilla peruviana* is from the Mediterranean and has large flower-heads, deep blue to violet. Easy to grow, these bulbs are very good in a mixed border and multiply readily. They have a short dormant season. *S. bifolia* is another good true gentian blue, and very hardy, flowering earlier than *S. peruviana*. *S. natalensis* is a giant on metre-long stems. It flowers in its second year. (Bluebells of English woods are now listed as *Endymion non-scriptus*.)

OTHER BULBS WITH BLUE FLOWERS SUITABLE FOR BEDS AND BORDERS

Allium — ornamental onion	Endymion — bluebell
Anemone coronaria	Ipheion
Crocus	Moraea

Bulbs with pink or red flowers

COLCHICUM	◯
Autumn crocus	▲25 cm
Liliaceae	❖ Autumn

Edging the border in clumps and drifts, the autumn crocus is a delightful sight with its vivid rosy-pink-to-mauve flowers. *Colchicum autumnale* is the hardiest of all the species. It is good for naturalising too. Leave the bulbs in the ground and propagate from offsets.

DIERAMA	◯
Angel's fishing rod	▲2 m
Iridaceae	❖ Summer

Dierama are from South Africa and are a hardy lot. *Dierama pulcherrimum* is perhaps the best for the garden, with bell-shaped pink, mauve or blood-red flowers on long, graceful, arching stems. Dierama look well beside a garden feature such as a bird bath or sundial, or hovering over a pool. Against dark green-leaved shrubs they stand out also. The plants are easily raised from seed, and, once established, do not like being disturbed.

Anemone

VALLOTA	○
Scarborough lily	▲45 cm
Amaryllidaceae	❖ Summer

These lovely flowers do not grow well for everyone, yet if they like their position they will thrive and increase. Yet another South African, *Vallota speciosa* can be started in pots and placed in the border, or grown directly into gritty, well-drained soil. The flowers are flaming red and last well in water. They can take slight frosts, and like to be watered during the growing season. Disturbing them upsets their flowering. Increase by seeds or offsets. The Scarborough lily looks especially striking if grown amongst verbena of the same shade.

OTHER BULBS WITH PINK OR RED FLOWERS SUITABLE FOR BEDS AND BORDERS

Allium — ornamental onion	Lycoris — spider lily
Anemone coronaria	Nerine — spider lily
Crinum	Ranunculus
Crocus	Sprekelia — Jacobean lily
Gladiolus	Tritonia
Hyacinthus	Tulipa
Ixia	Veltheimia
Lilium	Watsonia — bugle lily

Bulbs with yellow and gold flowers

FRITILLARIA	◯◗
Liliaceae	▲Up to 1 m
	❖ Spring

Unfortunately fritillarias thrive only in cool areas. They are so beautiful it is worth giving them a go in areas with cold winters. Crown imperial, *Fritillaria imperialis*, is magnificent — most effective in the border with its stately stems and large, glowing amber bells. *F. imperialis* 'Lutea' has golden-yellow bells. You can grow fritillarias from seed, although they take their time to germinate — over a year sometimes — so it is really best to buy bulbs if you can get them. Well-drained soil and humus suit fritillarias, and they do not mind some shade.

STERNBERGIA	◯
Amarylliadaceae	▲20 cm
	❖ Autumn

Welcome in autumn when perennials are past their prime, *Sternbergia lutea* makes a good show in beds and borders. The flowers are a clean, clear, shiny yellow, most attractive at the foot of shrubs and when mingling with other subjects. Once planted, you can forget about them in the garden, for they are child's play to grow. Do not bother to lift sternbergias, but rest assured you will always have them, cheerfully flowering faithfully.

ZANTEDESCHIA	◯
Calla lily	▲25–50 cm
Araceae	❖ Spring–Summer

Calla lilies are much hybridised. Of the species, *Zantedeschia pentlandii* is perhaps the best yellow, a rich golden colour with a cute black patch at the base. These lilies from South Africa do particularly well in Australia because of the intense light which brings out their equally intense colours. They are not over particular, but can be grown in pots if the soil is heavy. The hybrids are available in some lovely warm colours, with the yellow and gold as attractive as any. Good as cut flowers too, calla lilies are exported to the Northern Hemisphere.

OTHER BULBS WITH YELLOW AND GOLD FLOWERS SUITABLE FOR BEDS AND BORDERS

Clivia — kaffir lily	Narcissus — daffodil
Crocus	Ranunculus
Freesia	Sandersonia
Lachenalia	Tritonia
Lilium	Tulipa

ANNUALS FOR BEDS AND BORDERS

Annuals are admirable for beds and borders, where they will quickly fill blank spaces with welcome colour. Most are easy to grow from seed. Sow or plant annuals in drifts of a single colour complementary to the adjacent shrubs and perennials. Sow in generous quantities as annual groundcover, choosing your varieties for scent and leaf texture as well as for their brilliance. Remove spent blooms to prolong the flowering period, but leave some flowerheads to self-seed.

Annuals with white flowers

COSMOS	○
Compositae	▲To 1 m
	❖ Summer

Cosmos bipinnatus 'Purity' has snow-white, anemone-like flowers on thin stems — they nod in the breeze, creating airy clouds in the border. Perfect for cutting, never needing dead-heading and cleaning up, cosmos are essential for the cottage garden. These paragons have pretty ferny foliage, come in pink and red, and often are bi-coloured. Water in hot weather, and propagate from seed.

LAVATERA	○
Mallow	▲60 cm
Malvaceae	❖ Summer

An outstanding annual, *Lavatera trimetris* comes in pink and white. The white variety, although delicate looking, is easy to grow and hardy. It makes a fine underplanting for roses. All mallows are easily propagated from seed.

SALVIA	○
Labiatae	▲50 cm
	❖ Summer–autumn

Although a perennial, *Salvia farinacea* is best grown as an annual. The white variety is outstanding, blending well with any other flowers. The silvery-white spikes last for months and are good for cutting. When the flowers finally drop a velvety-grey seedhead will last on the plant well into winter. Easily grown from seed, *S. farinacea* needs to be planted in clumps or drifts, try it with silver artemisias and blue salvia 'Victoria'.

OTHER ANNUALS WITH WHITE FLOWERS FOR BEDS AND BORDERS

Alcea — hollyhock (biennial)   Antirrhinum — snapdragon
Ammobium — winged everlasting   *Begonia semperflorens* — wax begonia

---

Cleome — spider flower
Consolida — larkspur
Digitalis — foxglove
Euphorbia — snow-on-the-mountain
Iberis — annual candytuft
Lobelia

Lobularia — alyssum
Nicotiana
Omphalodes linifolia
Papaver — opium poppy; shirley poppy
Petunia
Primula malacoides — fairy primula

Annuals with blue flowers

ANCHUSA	○
Boraginaceae	▲45 cm
	❖ Winter–spring

If you want intense, brilliant azure-blue forget-me-not-type flowers on strong stems, grow *Anchusa capensis*. It is valuable in the border when interspersed with perennials and planted under shrubs and roses. Self-seeding, *A. capensis* will always be a feature of your spring beds once you have introduced it. It is not fussy over soil as long as it is well drained.

NEMOPHILA	◑
Baby blue-eyes	▲15–25 cm
Hydrophyllaceae	❖ Spring–summer

Nemophila menziesii, an edging plant for beds and borders, is studded with open blue flowers with white centres. It does well in cool districts and is untroubled by pests, but does like a rich, well-drained, moist soil. Sow the seed direct into the planting position under shrubs or perennials. Baby blue-eyes looks particularly charming when grown amongst spring-flowering bulbs.

NIGELLA	○
Love-in-a-mist	▲45 cm
Ranunculaceae	❖ Spring–summer

Nigella damascena comes in shades of blue and is a delightfully light and airy plant to grow in beds and borders. Make successive sowings through spring in any spare garden pockets, where they are to flower. As long as the soil is well-drained, nigella will fill the gaps with sky-blue flowers and ferny fronds, followed by curiously shaped seedpods which dry well.

Annuals with pink or red flowers

ALCEA	○
Hollyhock	▲1–2.5 m
Malvaceae	❖ Summer

Biennial hollyhocks, *Alcea rosea*, are sunlovers and can be grown against a wall; in the border they will need staking. Subject to rust unfortunately, hollyhocks nevertheless are well worth persevering with. They make an admirable feature in a cottage garden. Rich soil suits them. Deep-pink and carmine-red hollyhocks are the most usual, although other colours are available. The large seeds germinate quickly and can be sown in boxes, for hollyhocks transplant readily.

CLEOME	○
Spider flower	▲1.5 m
Capparidaceae	❖ Summer–autumn

This robust bushy plant can get too exuberant, but is excellent for larger gardens and at the back of the border. *Cleome spinosa* has handsome pink, mauve or white airy, fragrant flowers. Best sown where they are to flower, cleomes need warmth and water. They come from the tropics, so do not sow them till late in spring.

MATTHIOLA	○
Stock	▲20–50 cm
Cruciferae	❖ Winter–summer

Favourite annuals, blooming from winter onwards, stocks have an intoxicating perfume and bonny flowers in pretty pastel colours. They need rich, well-drained soil and dislike windy conditions. The double varieties are best. Early flowering 'Austral' has double flowers of pink, red and white. Make successive sowings to ensure a long flowering period. Stocks can be temperamental — if they have a check in their growth, they sulk.

Annuals with yellow and gold flowers

CHEIRANTHUS	◯◗
Wallflower	▲20–60 cm
Cruciferae	❖ Winter–spring

Biennial wallflowers have pleasing autumn colours and a sweet fragrance. You can get them in separate colours. The cream, primrose, lemon, yellow and gold varieties are especially fine. Grow wallflowers in clumps in the border alongside bulbs in the same cheerful colours, e.g. narcissi.

LIMNANTHES	◯◗
Meadow foam	▲15 cm
Limnanthaceae	❖ Spring–summer

Limnanthes douglasii spreads in a charming fashion and is covered with buttery-yellow, white-tipped, shining flowers. Admirable for edgings, and fronts of borders, particularly if intermingled with blue *Nemophila menziesii* and spring-flowering bulbs, *L. douglasii* does not currently get the recognition it deserves.

VIOLA	◯◗
Pansy	▲15–30 cm
Violaceae	❖ Spring–winter

Pansies have blossomed out, and now come in quite startling colours, from soft pastels to brilliant gold. Hybrid pansies 'Mellow 21 F.1 Hybrid' have 21 different shades, including several luminous clear yellow, orange, apricot and gold colours amongst them. Easy to grow, pansies do better in cool climates. Propagate from seed.

OTHER ANNUALS WITH YELLOW AND GOLD FLOWERS SUITABLE FOR BEDS AND BORDERS

Antirrhinum — snapdragon

Calendula — pot marigold

Celosia — cockscomb; Prince of Wales feather

Eschscholzia — California poppy

Gomphrena — globe everlasting

Helichrysum — strawflower

Hibiscus trionum — New Zealand hibiscus

Papaver — Iceland poppy

Portulaca

Tagetes — African marigold; French marigold

Tropaeolum — nasturtium

Zinnia

ON THE
BOUNDARY

3

HEDGES • BOUNDARY FENCES • Shrubs for the fenceline • Climbers for boundary
fences and walls • Trees and shrubs for boundaries

On the boundary, barriers are often essential. Barriers keep animals
out and protect your own piece of paradise. ('Paradise' is thought to
be the old Persian word for park. The first Persian gardens provided
shade and privacy.)

Fences are a quickly made, functional boundary. Curtain your fences
with climbers and shrubs of special form, shape and colour. Hedges
form a solid and continuous barrier. If you live in the country you
could think of a ha-ha to keep animals out, and the view unimpaired.
Or you may want an informal and casual boundary with shrubs, not
delineated, just providing a hint of a demarcation line. However,
you must be very sure of your own boundary line. And always think
of the picture you wish to create, whether viewed from the street,
inside the house or from other main vantage points around the garden.

HEDGES

Hedges form compartments in the garden like rooms in a house, and help to make an area appear larger. Clipping trees and shrubs into shapes is one of the oldest forms of gardening. Topiary (from *toparius*, Latin for 'gardener') was fashionable in Roman times, and hedges are a form of topiary. Hedges are long walls, providing shade and seclusion, and forming a most effective boundary.

You can grow one type of plant to keep the hedge clipped and uniform, or grow a tapestry of different hedge plants in informal groups, using various sizes and colours. Good preparation of the soil is necessary; hedges are there for keeps. They need regular maintenance but provide excellent shelter and great character.

ABELIA	○
Caprifoliaceae	▲2 m
	❖ Spring–summer

Abelia x *grandiflora* makes a fine hedge, easily maintained. The flowers are dainty, pink and fragrant. Quick growing abelia is an old favourite for hedging, and is still one of the best. The plants like a warm, moist climate, and need spacing at least 25 cm apart. Cuttings root with ease.

ATRIPLEX	○
Salt bush	▲1.5 m
Chenopodiaceae	

A hardy Australian, impervious to sand, salt spray and wind, *Atriplex nummularia*, with pleasant grey foliage, is the most handsome of the species. It forms a shrub which is easily clipped and trained into a hedge, and is ideal in hot, dry situations. Propagate by cuttings — do not mist them. Atriplex do not even mind salty soils. Much work is being done in Australia on atriplex species as a food source for sheep in arid desert areas. *A. halimus* is another good species for a hedge.

BUXUS	○◐
Box	▲To 3 m
Buxaceae	

In Europe box hedges have been grown for centuries, framing parterres and knot gardens. Evergreen, hardy and versatile, plants of common box, *Buxus sempervirens*, can be clipped to a few centimetres or allowed to take their heads, in which case they will grow tall, and buxom with it. So amenable to clipping, box can be used for the fashionable topiary trees in tubs, or formed into shapes in the garden. Where a flowery hedge would be intrusive, a box hedge may suit. *B. sempervirens* 'Suffruticosa' is a smaller form. (Another hedge plant suitable for a knot garden is germander, *Teucrium fruticans* — an admirable plant with silver-grey foliage.)

CHAENOMELES ◯◐

Japonica	▲1.5 m
Rosaceae	❖ Winter–spring

The lovely *Chaenomeles sinensis* has eye-catching blossoms of white and pink through to red, and these flower at a time of year when most needed. Semi-deciduous, japonicas and the brilliant cultivars tolerate sand or clay and many different climate types. They form a dense hedge which makes a good front boundary. This shrub is easily clipped, but mind the thorns. The flowers are excellent for picking and the large fruits make delicious jelly. Propagate from seed and cuttings.

CHOISYA ◯◐

Mexican orange blossom	▲1 m
Rutaceae	❖ Spring

Choisya ternata is a well-loved shrub, and adaptable. It makes a fine hedge and is easily propagated from cuttings. The sweet, heavily scented white flowers cover the whole plant. This versatile shrub is at home in many places in the garden.

FEIJOA ◯

Myrtaceae	▲2 m
	❖ Late spring

Scrumptious autumn or winter fruit and attractive red flowers on grey-green foliage give *Feijoa sellowiana* an advantage as a hedge. Easily kept under control and not attacked much by pests and diseases, feijoas are good growing at the beach too. The more you feed them, the bigger the fruit and larger will grow your hedge. Feijoas are often planted as shelter belts for orchards.

GUAVA ◯

Myrtaceae	▲3 m
	❖ Summer

Guava, *Psidium cattleianum*, is another admirable hedge plant for warm gardens. A low-growing and attractive hedge can be made with *Ugni molinae*, Chilean guava or cranberry, which has small delicious red fruit, suitable for jam making.

LAVANDULA ◯

Lavender	▲1–1.5 m
Labiatae	❖ All year

Lavender hedges are deservedly popular and delight with their fragrance. Easily clipped, several varieties are suitable for a hedge, fronting the road or to screen off the vegetable or herb garden — a boundary between the ornamental and the off the vegetable or herb garden — a boundary between the ornamental and the culinary. Fresh lavender, *Lavandula dentata* does well in warmer areas generally and the common lavender, *L. angustifolia* (syn. *L. spica*) likes cooler conditions.

Many lavender hybrids are available and collectors will want all the coloured varieties. 'Hidcote Blue' is opulently dark. Dwarf 'Alba Nana' is white and richly scented, and 'Rosa Nana' is prettily pink.

Trim off lavender heads after flowering and cut back. (The flowers are useful for pot pourri.) Lavenders will thrive in any gritty, well-drained soil. Propagate from cuttings or seed.

PHOTINIA ○

Rosaceae ▲2 m

❖ Spring

Photinia glabra 'Rubens' is an old favourite for hedges, and no wonder. Photinias are renowned for their handsome red-to-Titian-red leaves. *P.* 'Red Robin' has the most intense foliage of all, the new leaves opening a brilliant red. Photinias enjoy being cut back as this encourages new growth. The flowers are insignificant. This hedge plant will grow in clay soil and is no trouble. Propagate from cuttings.

OTHER SHRUBS AND TREES SUITABLE FOR HEDGES

Bougainvillea
Buddleia salvifolia — butterfly bush
Callistemon — bottlebrush
Camellia sasanqua
Casuarina — sheoke
Coprosma repens — mirror plant
Corokia
Correa — Australian fuchsia
Escallonia
Fagus — beech
Fuchsia magellanica
Griselinia — broadleaf
Hibiscus
Hydrangea

Lonicera nitida — hedge honeysuckle
Myrtus — common myrtle
Nerium — oleander
Phebalium
Pittosporum
Rhaphiolepis — Indian hawthorn
Rosa — floribunda type
Rosmarinus — rosemary
Syzygium — rose apple; lilly pilly
Tecomaria — tecoma
Vaccinium — blueberry
Virgilia

BOUNDARY FENCES

Fences are easy and quick to build, and prove an effective barrier on a front boundary or between neighbours. A picket fence is attractive in front of a cottage or villa. A high wooden paling fence baffles traffic noise, and is sensible where privacy is needed. You must be sure of the boundary when building a fence. In some areas there may be local council regulations restricting height or building materials, etc.

You can grow shrubs on the fenceline, or climbers. Different types of plants are needed for different styles of fences, either open or solid.

TOP LEFT: Clever use of conifers defines the boundary between the house and drive in a restrained but effective way.

LEFT: For a country look, roses and perennials complement the house in this rural setting.

BELOW: A curved hedge of dwarf grey-leaved hebes contrasts most desirably with neighbouring plants.

RIGHT: *A path with all the ingredients for success: a path to beckon you on enticingly, with an air of secrecy; edges softened by plants, and framed by the old-fashioned clematis 'Nellie Moser'.*

BELOW: *Fragrant herbs soften and enhance informal steps made from old railway sleepers.*

Shrubs for the fenceline

You may want a screen of shrubs against the fence. The clean, sharp lines of modern homes look best with shrubs having strong architectural lines. Cottage gardens call for flowering shrubs and romantic climbers.

When planting trees and shrubs, follow a plan. One species planted in a group or drift can look more effective than many different types dotted about — 'cocktail planting'. Height, shape and aspect must be considered.

ABUTILON	○◑
Chinese lantern	▲3 m
Malvaceae	❖ All year

Abutilons are well suited to growing against wooden walls and fences. Popular modern varieties are mainly hybrids in colours from paper white, cream, lemon through orange to deepest red. *Abutilon megapotamicum* has enchanting pendulous red and yellow flowers which show to advantage against a solid background. Any well-drained soil suits Chinese lantern shrubs and you can grow them very easily from cuttings. Birds are attracted to the flowers — to watch a tiny silver-eye upside down gathering nectar is reason enough to grow abutilons.

Abutilon

FREMONTODENDRON	○
Fremontia	▲2 m
Bombacaceae	❖ Spring–summer

Fremontodendron californicum and *F. mexicanum* are cheerful shrubs with dull green, attractively shaped leaves and bright, long-lasting flat yellow flowers. Although easily grown, they dislike wind and wet soil and are particularly suited to growing against a wooden fence. Fremontias are unusual shrubs and pleasing to grow.

NANDINA	○◖●●
Sacred bamboo	▲1 m
Berberidaceae	❖ Spring

Nandina domestica is a very ornamental and unique plant to grow. It has graceful pink-to-red foliage on bamboo-like stems and modest white flowers followed by bright red berries. The foliage turns brilliant apricot to red colours in autumn and winter. *N. domestica* 'Pygmaea' is a dwarf variety with multi-coloured foliage and is very popular. You need to plant several for effect, perhaps in a group next to other shrubs. These dwarf nandina take up little room and look at their best against a fence.

PYRACANTHA	○
Fire thorn	▲2 m
Rosaceae	❖ Spring–summer

Espalier subjects are excellent against paling fences and walls. *Pyracantha angustifolia* has orange berries produced right along the branches in late autumn and winter, and is most satisfying espaliered against a natural wood or brown fence, and on a white one too. Yellow and red-berried varieties are also available, and are just as stunning. The many *Pyracantha* species are easily propagated from cuttings, but mind the prickles.

REINWARDTIA	○
Linaceae	▲90 cm
	❖ Winter

Shrubs flowering in winter are always welcome, and the bold yellow flowers of *Reinwardtia indica* are glowingly warm against the deep green foliage. *R. indica* does very well against a warm solid wall or fence where it appreciates the heat. This shrub takes up little room, being small and neat, and is compatible with a group of Vireya rhododendrons, for example.

RHODODENDRON	○
Vireya	▲1–1.5 m
Ericaceae	❖ Year round

Vireya rhododendrons are an excellent, fairly recent introduction to our gardens. Quite unlike their cooler-climate cousins, Vireyas bear flowers in warm, autumn colours. Against a brown wooden fence they look very well indeed.

These rhododendrons are from New Guinea and Borneo in particular, and so are unused to much change in the seasons. An equable climate is necessary for them. Most Vireyas flower at least twice annually, and if you have a collection, one or other will be out at some time during the year. There are dozens to choose from, and Vireyas are well suited to container culture, especially in areas with cool winters. Feed them with liquid fertilisers and compost, remembering that, like all rhododendrons, they must have acid soil.

OTHER SHRUBS SUITABLE FOR GROWING AGAINST FENCES AND WALLS

Boronia	Fuchsia (espalier)
Bouvardia	*Hibiscus rosa-sinensis* and hybrids
Camellia	*Jasminum mesnyii*
Clerodendrum — blue butterfly bush	Luculia
	Mahonia
Euphorbia — poinsettia	Rosa
Fatsia japonica — aralia	*Serruria florida* — blushing bride
Fruit trees (espalier)	*Stachyurus praecox*

Climbers for boundary fences and walls

Climbers are practical to grow against fences and walls. Vertical space is all they require, and this makes them well-suited to smaller gardens. Climbers can be regarded as curtains and blinds to decorate a fence, adding colour and texture. They climb in different ways, some attaching themselves to supports by aerial roots, others twining. Those twiners suitable for growing on picket fences and other open fences are marked with an asterisk*.

CLEMATIS	○◗
Ranunculaceae	▲To 4 m
	❖ Spring–summer

A large family with over 250 species, clematis are suitable for growing against solid fences as long as they have a cool root run. Some varieties are vigorous and prefer to grow up amongst shrubs and trees.

The large-flowered hybrid clematis are admirable grown against a wooden fence or wall, provided the position is away from wind and is not dry, nor in the sun for the hottest part of the day. Of the species, C. *macropetala*, a deciduous climber from China, is good against a cool fence. It has mauve flowers and attractive foliage.

Try C. *cirrhosa*, an evergreen with bell-shaped creamy flowers. The range of large-flowered hybrids is so great it is best to see them in bloom before making a selection. Watch out for slugs and snails on young growth. Propagate by fresh seed or by cuttings.

MACFADYENA*	○
Cat's paw	▲8 m
Bignoniaceae	❖ Late spring–summer

If you want a dazzling yellow trumpet-flowered climber, and have a warm position, *Macfadyena unguis-cati* (syn. *Doxantha unguis-cati*) is for you. It is evergreen in these conditions, but loses its leaves in cool climates, although it will withstand slight frosts. The cat's paw is a vigorous climber and useful against a large fence, or growing up a tree. It should be cut back each year to curtail its rampant growth.

PANDOREA*	○
Bower of beauty	▲3 m
Bignoniaceae	❖ Spring–autumn

The Australian evergreen bower of beauty, *Pandorea jasminoides*, has white flowers. Watch out for the cultivar 'Lady Di' — it is quite lovely. 'Bower of Beauty' is also delightful, having delicate ice-cream-pink blooms with a magenta-to-wine throat. This climber's foliage is attractive and the plant is easily controlled. Give it well-drained soil and a warm position and it will flower for months. Wonga wonga vine, *P. pandorana*, is a different proposition. Covered in creamy flowers and light green foliage, it is better for a large area as it grows alarmingly fast if it is happy. Hardier than *P. jasminoides*, the wonga wonga vine is better for cool areas.

Propagate the pandorea by tip cuttings in late summer or autumn.

PARTHENOCISSUS	○◗
Boston ivy; Virginia creeper	▲To 20 m
Vitaceae	

Be very careful where you plant this vigorous climber — some varieties have been known to soar 30 metres high — but they do have their uses. Boston ivy, *Parthenocissus tricuspidata*, is semi-evergreen in all but the coldest situations. The glorious rich scarlet of its leaves in autumn is breathtaking. The cultivar 'Veitchii' has a more compact form of growth and smaller leaves.

Virginia creeper, *P. quinquefolia*, is very hardy and will grow to 20 metres. Chinese virginia creeper, *P. henryana*, is slow growing and its deep-green velvety leaves with bold white veins turn brilliant colours in autumn. On long fences or solid brick walls these creepers are excellent. They all do better out of the strongest afternoon sun.

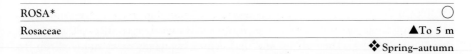

ROSA*　　　　　　　　　　　　　　　　　　　　　　　○

Rosaceae　　　　　　　　　　　　　　　　　　　　▲To 5 m

❖ Spring–autumn

The old-fashioned climbing roses are charming attached to pickets or growing up and along a paling fence. All you have to decide is what colour you require and there's sure to be a climbing rose available. Climbing roses include 'Handel', rosy-pink edged cream; 'Mermaid', single yellow; 'Black boy', deep crimson and 'Wedding Day'.

OTHER CLIMBERS TO GROW ON FENCES AND WALLS

Actinidia kolomikta　　　　　　　　Pelargonium — climbing geranium;
Bougainvillea　　　　　　　　　　　　ivy-leaved geranium
Cobaea — Cathedral bells　　　　　　Pyrostegia — golden shower
Ficus pumila — creeping fig　　　　Rhodochiton — purple bells
Hedera — ivy　　　　　　　　　　　　*Solanum wendlandii* — blue potato
Hoya carnosa — wax plant　　　　　vine
Lonicera — honeysuckle　　　　　　　Thunbergia
Passiflora — passionflower　　　　　*Trachelospermum jasminoides* —
　　　　　　　　　　　　　　　　　　Chinese star jasmine

Trees and shrubs for boundaries

Perhaps you do not want a definite boundary of a fence or hedge between neighbours or on your road frontage. You may prefer informal groups of trees and shrubs set in a communal area. You could consider fruit trees to share — edible ornamentals — or you may decide on a theme of Australian natives (see Chapter 12), but whatever your choice, go for repeat plantings to achieve maximum impact and serenity. Select your trees and shrubs to complement your house design and the predominant style and character of your street.

Whatever your choice, you will not want to plant large trees which may give too much shade to you and your neighbours. A mature height of 10 metres would be the absolute maximum for trees in a suburban garden. Allow plenty of room between each for width-ways growth and underplant carefully. Deciduous varieties often annoy people when they have to remove leaves from gutters or rake them off lawns and paths. However, if shelter and screening is not a priority, think of more open-growing varieties, e.g. prunus and maples (see Chapter 5).

AZARA　　　　　　　　　　　　　　　　　　　　○◐

Flacourtiaceae　　　　　　　　　　　　　　　　▲4 m

❖ Late winter–spring

Azara microphylla, from Chile, is a handsome, upright, small evergreen tree, ideal on a boundary. It has modest yellow flowers and neat and shiny little leaves. The strong vanilla scent from the flowers more than makes up for their insignificance. A spray of *A. microphylla* will scent an entire room with its fragrance. Other species are worthwhile too, their shape and dark leaves complementing many shrubs in a satisfying way. *A. integrifolia* has bright yellow flowers; *A. lanceolata* is elegant, producing light-mauve berries. The azaras all appreciate acid soil, compost and leaf mould, and are hardy.

BANKSIA	○
Proteaceae	▲2–6 m
	❖ Winter–spring

Tough banksias will thrive in light, well-drained soils in open situations. *Banksia ericifolia* always looks attractive, and has large bottlebrush flowers of deep orange with scarlet tips. Winter-flowering *B. grandis* boasts large, deeply-cut leaves and spikes of yellow flower-cones, often 30 cm long. *B. coccinea* is outstanding, with fat red flowerheads, and does well in dry climates — it does not care for humidity. All banksia flowers are fine for cutting and are long lasting, and birds visit them for the nectar. Grow banksias with other Australian natives such as grevilleas, to which they are related. (See p.112.)

CHAMAECYPARIS	○◗
False cypress	▲7 m
Cupressaceae	

Ornamental and evergreen, grown for its blue-green foliage and handsome shape, hardy *Chamaecyparis lawsoniana* 'Allumii' is very good for a cool garden. It makes a useful accent, and looks well planted with smaller, round-shaped shrubs. 'Fletcheri' is more compact but has the same columnar habit. Some cultivars have fern-like foliage, and others are tinted with yellow.(*Cupressus* (see p. 70) are the cypress species to grow in warmer climates.)

CITRUS	○
Meyer lemon	▲To 1.5 m
Rutaceae	❖ Autumn–winter

Highly ornamental, but the least demanding of all the citrus, Meyer lemons are good to share with a neighbour. The fruit is always welcome and the flower scent as intense as any orange blossom. Well-drained soil is essential, previously worked and enriched. Citrus need water in summer and regular feeding in autumn and spring. Keep mulched, and clear of encroaching lawn or plants for best results. Citrus do not need much in the way of pruning. Whilst trees are small, protect them from frost with a covering. A mandarin ('Imperial' or 'Emperor' are popular cultivars) planted with your lemon is a good idea if the climate is suitable.

LEPTOSPERMUM	○◑
Manuka; teatree	▲To 2 m
Myrtaceae	❖ Autumn–spring

For a front boundary or borders with neighbours, the hardy *Leptospermum scoparium* and its hybrids are most useful and decorative with their white-to-red, long-lasting flowers and fragrant foliage. Of the many cultivars available, some of the best are 'Coconut Ice', 'Red Damask' and 'Lambethii', with flowers of crimson to deep red, and the hardy, pink-flowering 'Keatleyi'. These are outstanding shrubs for many places in the garden, provided the soil has good drainage.

PROTEA	○
Proteaceae	▲1–2.5 m
	❖ Winter–spring

As long as your soil has good drainage and sun, you should be able to grow a beautiful protea or two. Magnificent flowering shrubs from an outstanding family, proteas number over 100 species. Hardy, striking *Protea neriifolia* will do well on a boundary. The king protea, *P. cynaroides*, has the largest flowers of any protea, but is a low-branching shrub best planted in conjunction with taller species. *P. laurifolia* produces striking flowers of shiny pink with feathery black tips, similar to *P. neriifolia*, and it flowers almost all year long. Proteas are dust resistant, making them ideal for front boundaries, and their foliage stays attractive too.

OTHER TREES AND SHRUBS SUITABLE FOR BOUNDARIES

Callistemon — bottlebrush
Camellia
Cupressus sempervirens 'Stricta'
    and 'Swane's Golden' — Italian
    cypress
Grevillea
Hibiscus syriacus

Hydrangea
Macadamia
Pittosporum
Pseudopanax — lancewood
Rhododendron
Syzygium — lilly pilly; rose apple
Virgilia

PAVING THE WAY

4

Paths are a necessary part of a garden. They provide access and character. Straight paths may accent a garden's design, but it must be remembered that there are no straight lines in nature. Curved and winding paths are more pleasing and fit more naturally into the landscape, and winding paths beckon invitingly.

Paths must be well made, with a firm foundation and non-slip surfaces. Interesting materials include bricks, slate, gravel, shells, concrete, tiles and timber. Your choice will be partly dictated by the style of your garden and house. It is preferable for a path to be of two-person width, making it roomy enough for wheelbarrow use.

Paving is an extra floor in the garden. Many materials can be used for paving. Slate, concrete slabs, bricks, flagstones, old concrete paths broken up and retrieved — all make fine paving.

Steps should be as simple as possible, to enable you to walk quickly from one level to another. Many materials can be used, adding charm, interest and character to the garden. Use the same materials as for the paths, or something similar. Try and make steps wide and shallow, rather than high and skimpy.

PATHS

Planting along paths is important for plants soften paths' edges and provide fragrance and beauty. Never grow plants with prickles or spiky leaves near a path's edge; leaf-shedding plants should be avoided too, for obvious reasons.

Shrubs for bordering paths

Small shrubs with scented leaves or flowers are the best for bordering paths. Slow-growing evergreen shrubs need little maintenance. Deciduous shrubs may shed their leaves all over the path. The shrubs described here are evergreen.

ADENANDRA	○
Rutaceae	▲60 cm–1 m
	❖ Late winter–summer

Adenandra fragrans is a neat little evergreen shrub with bright, rosy, five-petalled flowers covering the tidy bush. The shiny leaves are aromatic. Slightly larger is *A. uniflora.* Its flowers, porcelain-white, backed pink, bloom for many months. Plant adenandras in groups.

ARTEMISIA	○
Compositae	▲To 1 m

Artemisias are perennial herbs, shrubs and sub-shrubs. *Artemisia absinthium* is a sub-shrub with silver filigree leaves and astringent scent. Most artemisias like light, well-drained soil. Artemisias are a great foil for riotous-coloured companions. Other shrub artemisias are also worth growing by a path. Try southernwood, *A. abrotanum,* but prune back annually to at least one-third of original size to keep it compact. Propagate from cuttings.

BORONIA	○◗
Rutaceae	▲1–1.3 m
	❖ Late winter–spring

There are over 70 species of boronia and all are Australian. They all prefer a light, acid, well-drained soil. One of the prettiest is *Boronia heterophylla,* which is covered in fuchsia-coloured bells. It has a lengthy flowering period and the blooms are good for cutting. Look out for the new hybrids. *B. megastigma* is the strongly scented one — its fragrance cannot be bettered, and what curious, brown, cup-shaped flowers it has. One or two shrubs will scent the entire garden. Many species have pink, open flowers, and many are perfumed. Propagate from seed.

DAPHNE ◯◖

Thymelaeaceae ▲To 1 m

❖ Winter–spring

Daphne odora, with its tight pink and white flowers, distributes a heady fragrance all winter. Daphne is well behaved and requires acid soil, well-drained. *D. odora* and its cultivars remain the favourites to grow, but others are worthwhile. *D. cneorum* is bushy, and has clusters of pink flowers. *D. x burkwoodii* forms a low, rounded shrub with bunches of pink flowers along its branches.

OXYPETALUM ◯

Asclepiadaceae ▲To 1 m

❖ Summer–autumn

Oxypetalum caeruleum (syn. *Tweedia caerulea*) has flowers of an astonishing colour, one unique to this small sub-shrub — a greyish-blue with brilliant deep-blue centre. The leaves are grey-green, felted and downy. Tweedia demands a mild climate and well-drained soil, and looks particularly well with deep blue or pink flowering plants. It will grow from cuttings but propagates easily from seed.

> OTHER SHRUBS SUITABLE FOR BORDERING PATHS
>
> | | |
> |---|---|
> | Azalea — evergreen types | Grevillea — groundcover types |
> | Buxus — common box | Hebe |
> | *Ceanothus* 'Blue Gem' | Lavandula — dwarf lavender |
> | Cistus — rock rose (small hybrids) | *Podalyria sericea* — satin bush |
> | *Convolvulus cneorum* | *Potentilla fruticosa* — cinquefoil |
> | *Deutzia* 'Nikko' | Santolina — lavender cotton |
> | Erica | Teucrium — germander |

Perennials for along the path

We are spoilt for choice when considering perennials suitable to edge and soften paths, so we must look for particular qualities. The selection mainly depends on position, soil and individual preferences. It is important to think in terms of foliage as well as flowers and fragrance. Many perennials included in other chapters are suitable for growing at a path's edge.

DIANTHUS ◯

Pinks ▲40 cm

Carophyllaceae ❖ Spring–summer

The lovely old pinks have a delicious scent of cloves. *Dianthus plumarius* is the main parent of the cottage pinks, some being lacy, others fringed. They come in white, pink, rose and carmine. The variety 'Mrs Sinkins', with double white flowers, scents the air around her, and is an ideal edging for a path, blooming for months on end. Undemanding old-fashioned pinks like sun, lime and good drainage. Propagate them from cuttings.

EPIMEDIUM	◯◑●
Berberidaceae	▲20–30 cm
	❖ Summer

Good for edging shady paths, evergreen *Epimedium pinnatum* looks especially well bordering brick or stone paths. Its heart-shaped, showy leaves, heavily veined, are in pleasant shades, deepening to red in autumn. The flowers are incidental, but are prettily shaped, small, yellow and waxy. All the species are hardy and worth growing, provided you have moist soil. *E.* x *rubrum* is a good hybrid with crimson flowers and leaves of deepest red in autumn. Others have white, pink or lilac flowers. Epemediums are good as groundcover under shrubs. Propagate from divisions.

HEUCHERA	◯◑
Coral bells	▲30–60 cm
Saxifragaceae	❖ Spring–summer

Heuchera sanguinea and its many varieties and hybrids flourish at the edge of an informal path. The foliage is always attractive, and the flowers are daintily produced on slender, arching stems. The flowers are good for cutting, too. The hybrids have white and pink to deep red flowers. Heuchera are increased from seed or division.

Impatiens

SEDUM	○
Stonecrop	▲ 10–20 cm
Crassulaceae	❖ Spring

Tough succulents, sedums grow quickly in many areas of the garden, and are culti-vated mostly for their unusual fleshy leaves, most interesting in texture, shape and colour. Bordering a path, *Sedum rubrotinctum*, with leaves like fat jellybeans and flowers of glistening yellow, is a great asset. Many sedums are mat-forming and a logical choice for a path's edge, especially where the soil is poor. Sedums are con-genial plants and are often dismissed just because they are so easy. Any stem cut-ting takes, and they always look good.

VERBENA	○
Verbenaceae	▲ 15–40 cm
	❖ Summer–autumn

Verbenas are exuberant bloomers, and very showy. They soften path edges and flower for months at a time, in a wide colour range, from white to purple. They are low-growing and spread quickly in sunny, dry places. Verbenas do get downy mildew, but apart from that are pretty healthy. *Verbena* x *hybrida* are the garden varieties grown for their large round flowerheads. Verbenas are increased by seed or cuttings.

OTHER PERENNIALS SUITABLE FOR GROWING BY PATHS

Alchemilla — lady's mantle
Anthemis — chamomile
Arabis — rock cress
Armeria — thrift; sea pink
Artemisia
Aster — Michaelmas daisy
Brachycome multifida
Campanula — bellflower
Cerastium — snow-in-summer
Chrysanthemum frutescens;
   C. hosmariense
C. parthenium — feverfew
Erigeron karvinskianus — babies' tears
Felicia amelloides — blue marguerite
Heliotropium — cherry pie, heliotrope
Iberis — perennial candytuft
Impatiens — busy Lizzie
Nierembergia repens
Thymus — thyme

Annuals for edging paths

Most annuals are but a temporary decoration, and can be time-consuming, but there are exceptions. A few annuals are carefree, and almost indispensable. These splendid plants are ideal for edging paths, and are renowned for their long flowering season, sparkle and colour.

LOBELIA	$\bigcirc\,\bigcirc$
Campanulaceae	▲10 cm
	❖ Spring–autumn

Lobelia erinus is known for its beautiful blue flowers, from sky-blue to deepest cobalt. New lobelias are appearing in colours from white to purple, some trailing, some compact. If they like their position, lobelias will reward you with flowers for six months. Grow them in a cool place. Every seed you sow will germinate.

RESEDA	$\bigcirc$
Mignonette	▲30–45 cm
Resedaceae	❖ Spring–summer

Mignonette, *Reseda odorata*, is grown for its tantalising perfume, its flowers being disappointing. The modest green blooms attract bees though, and the delicious scent attracts us. Easily grown in lime-enriched soil, mignonette is best in drifts or bunches edging the path, not in a line. Mignonette is a worthwhile annual to grow in pots. *R. alba* is a taller variety with white flowers.

VIOLA	$\bigcirc\,\bigcirc$
Violaceae	▲10 cm
	❖ Spring–summer

Violas, although perennials, are best treated as annuals. *Viola cornuta* is a fine mauve-flowered variety which makes a superb edging. Dwarf and compact, violas have flowers from white to wine, with lemon, yellow and apricot shades as well, and many colour combinations. Violas like moist, cool soil. Pansies, too, are ideal for edging paths.

OTHER ANNUALS SUITABLE FOR GROWING BY PATHS

Ageratum
Begonia semperflorens — wax begonia
Brachycome iberidifolia — Swan River daisy
Cosmos
Dianthus — pinks
Limnanthes douglasii — meadow foam
Linaria — toad flax
Lobularia — sweet alyssum
Nemophila — baby blue-eyes
Petunia hybrids
Phlox drummondii
Primula malacoides — fairy primula
Salpiglossis sinuata

PAVING

Paving has crevices and cracks, ideal for growing plants in, to soften the appearance. Plants oblivious to being ill-treated and trodden on are the best to use here, also plants exuding a pleasant smell when crushed. The paved area may be used to dine al fresco, or be part of the barbecue area, so tender plants are tabu, although some may be planted on the perimeter.

Perennials for use in paved areas

A cool root run under the paving and warmth on top provides almost perfect conditions for many perennial plants. Restrict the colours used so all the plants blend with one another, and leave plenty of room between them for ease of walking. The perennials recommended here can be walked upon, but only lightly. Restrained planting is necessary.

ANTHEMIS	○
Chamomile	▲25 cm
Compositae	❖ Spring

Anthemis nobilis (syn. Chamaemelum nobile) is often used as an alternative to a lawn. In between paving crevices it works very well. Shear it back if it grows too tall. The non-flowering variety is perhaps the best to grow. It has fragrant leaves when crushed and is very hardy. Chamomiles are not troubled by pests and diseases and are easily propagated by division.

ARENARIA	○◗
Sandwort	▲2.5–15 cm
Caryophyllaceae	❖ Spring–summer

Arenaria balearica does not mind being walked on every now and then, and tolerates shade. Its flowers are white and starry. A. montana forms a dense mat, produces myriad white flowers and enjoys sun. Gritty or sandy soil suits these plants best.

MENTHA	◗
Mint	▲2.5 cm
Labiatae	❖ Summer

Most mints are too rampant for paving planting, but jewel mint, Mentha requienii, forms a close mat and is deliciously aromatic when crushed underfoot. It is easily grown, and has tiny purple flowers. Cool, moist soils suit this mint from Corsica and Sardinia.

PHLOX	○
Moss phlox	▲10–15 cm
Polemoniaceae	❖ Spring–summer

Phlox subulata forms a mat of green, decorated with small white, pink, red or purple flowers, and is an excellent subject for growing in between paving. Cut back after flowering. Grow *P. subulata* with thyme. Propagate from cuttings.

SOLEIROLIA	○◖
Baby's tears	▲10–15 cm
Urticaceae	❖ Spring–summer

Soleirolia soleirolii (syn. *Helxine soleirolii*) is an evergreen, moss-like plant which forms a green velvet carpet in paving cracks, provided the paving is in shade or part-shade. The flowers are inconspicuous.

THYMUS	○
Thyme	▲10–25 cm
Labiatae	❖ Spring–summer

Thymes are admirable for use in paving and on steps, their habit neat, their leaves fragrant. Prostrate or creeping thyme, *Thymus serpyllum*, covers quickly, producing carpets of colour in pinks, white or red. *T. praecox* has pretty pink-to-mauve flowers in spring. Other varieties have flowers in purple, pink and red too — oriental rugs in the garden. Bees visit thyme flowers, so do not walk barefoot on the paving.

OTHER PERENNIALS SUITABLE FOR GROWING IN PAVED AREAS

Ajuga — bugle
Armeria — thrift; sea pink
Aubrieta
Cotula
Dianthus gratianopolitanus —
    Cheddar pink

Helianthemum — rock rose
Iberis — perennial candytuft
Lewisia
Linaria alpina — toad flax
Nierembergia repens
Pratia angulata
Raoulia australis

Annuals for paved areas

Annuals are a temporary measure when used in paving, but several are well worthwhile. Although most annuals have a short life, it is a colourful one.

Specimen trees enhance the entranceways of these properties.

RIGHT: *Autumn and spring produce equally dramatic displays from the deck in a temperate climate garden.*

BELOW: *Pots and palms, pergola and pool create an inviting holiday spirit in this low-maintenance garden of subtropical plants.*

ANAGALLIS	○
Pimpernel	▲ 15–25 cm
Primulaceae	❖ Summer–autumn

Anagallis linifolia is a perennial best treated as an annual. Brilliant blue blooms cover the plant for many months. Easily grown from seed sown directly into paving cracks, pimpernel is a hardy plant.

LOBULARIA	○
Sweet alyssum	▲ 10 cm
Cruciferae	❖ Year round

Lobularia maritima can be grown in many places in the garden, and once you have it, you have it for always. 'Carpet of Snow' hugs the ground; 'Rosie O'Day' spreads quickly and lives up to its name. Alyssum leaves a faint honey fragrance in the air. For edges or in paving it is as perfect an annual as you will get.

MALCOMIA	○
Virginia stock	▲ 15–30 cm
Cruciferae	❖ Spring

A most precocious plant, *Malcomia maritima* flowers within weeks of sowing, and is invaluable for quick fill-ins. The dainty flowers in baby pastel colours are sweetly scented. Sow where they are to bloom. Virginia stock is self-seeding.

PORTULACA	○
Portulaceae	▲ 20 cm
	❖ Summer

With succulent leaves, portulaca creeps happily between crevices in paving. *P. grandiflora* has pretty, rose-like double flowers and is a kaleidoscope of colour. Portulaca does not really take kindly to being trodden on.

OTHER ANNUALS SUITABLE FOR GROWING IN PAVED AREAS

Iberis — annual candytuft
Linaria — annual toad flax
Lobelia

Mesembryanthemum —
Livingstone daisy

STEPS

Plants enhance and soften the straight outlines of steps. If a handrail is needed, a climber growing over it looks attractive. Shrubs and perennials suitable for bordering paths (p. 58) and for banks (see Chapter 1, p. 12) are those to use at the side of steps. Here are a few other suggestions.

Perennials for growing beside steps

CYMBALARIA	◐
Ivy-leaved toad flax	▲5 cm
Scrophulariaceae	❖ Spring–summer

Cymbalaria muralis grows in a modest fashion, with tiny, mauve-white snapdragon-type flowers. It looks delicate but is as tough as old boots. Once you have it, you always will. *C. muralis* will trail along the back of steps and not get in the way.

ERIGERON	○
Babies' tears	▲15–25 cm
Compositae	❖ Year round

Erigeron karvinskianus (syn. *E. mucronatus*) will clamber down the side of steps in a carefree manner. It is useful throughout the garden and seldom stops flowering, always looking good, winter and summer, rain or shine. The sweet, simple, daisy flowers are pink and white. *E. karvinskianus* fulfils many roles in the garden. Always amiable, it tumbles down walls, grows very well in pots and hanging baskets, makes a delightful groundcover and is a vital ingredient of the cottage garden. Make sure you have it somewhere.

HELIOTROPIUM	◐
Cherry pie; heliotrope	▲30–60 cm
Boraginaceae	❖ Summer

At the side of steps bushy heliotrope softens outlines and produces its delicious fragrance for passersby. *Heliotropium arborescens* (syn. *H. peruvianum*) is an old-fashioned flower enjoying popularity with the cottage garden renaissance. Its white, blue or purple blooms are strongly and sweetly scented, and good for cutting. Any well-drained soil suits heliotrope, and it is quickly increased by cuttings. In cold districts it is usually treated as an annual.

HETEROCENTRON	◐
Heeria; Spanish shawl	▲Prostrate
Melostomataceae	❖ Year round

The pretty little prostrate plant, *Heterocentron elegans*, creeps over steps, and can be persuaded to keep off the parts to be walked on. It has tiny, dark-green leaves, and on and off during the year is covered completely in cyclamen flowers. It will stand slight frosts, and will grow in poor soil. Propagate from division.

OTHER PERENNIALS SUITABLE FOR GROWING BY STEPS

Alchemilla — lady's mantle
Campanula — bellflower
Chrysanthemum frutescens —
    marguerite
Convolvulus mauritanicus
Echevaria
Geum

Pelargonium — ivy-leaved
    geranium; climbing geranium
Phormium — New Zealand flax
    (small cultivars)
Saxifraga
Sedum — stonecrop
Vinca — periwinkle

FIRST
IMPRESSIONS

5

Trees and shrubs for gateways and specimen plantings

First impressions are most important, and the entranceway from the street to your property is your invitation to callers. And when you yourself arrive home, your spirits should lift as you see your house and garden come into view. Usually your entranceway will be the focal point of the front garden, and its style should be complementary to this and the house. You may choose a wide, formal but welcoming gate with cypress sentinels either side, a romantic lattice under an archway festooned with roses, or grand wrought-iron gates flanked by palms. Conversely, you may need an entrance in a style to maintain your privacy. Whatever you desire, plants will improve and embellish the entrance to your home.

Your entranceway may also give access for cars. Driveways must be kept clear of overhanging branches, and at street level shrubs or trees which might obscure a motorist's vision when reversing should be avoided.

The front door is the entranceway to the house and should repeat the welcoming impression created at the front gate. It is also the focal point of the house's street face, more often than not, and lends itself to imaginative treatment. It is practical to have shrubs and trees in pots and containers here. Often the front door is protected by a porch and eaves of the house; nearby plants directly in the ground might suffer from lack of water or inadequate soil. Container-grown subjects add drama and colour to the front-door area, can be changed with the seasons and create interest in unique ways.

Large bonsai trees in dragon pots are attractive beside a formal door. The traditional clipped bay tree, *Laurus nobilis*, in a Versailles tub is just right in a doorway of classical styling. Barrels spilling over with geraniums, daisies, erigeron, or other dainty perennials enhance the informal atmosphere of an old-fashioned cottage entrance.

Trees and shrubs for gateways and specimen plantings

Trees and shrubs for gateways and accents in the front garden need to be compatible with your house style, relate well to your street setting, complement the front hedge or fence and be intrinsic to the overall design of your garden.

See what other people are growing in your area. Large, spreading trees generally will not do. Trees with graceful columns are better, or species to train, such as weeping cherries or the classical cypress. Trees which make a strong statement at one or more seasons of the garden year are the specimens to look out for.

ARCHONTOPHOENIX	◑
Alexander palm, bangalow palm	▲ To 8 m
Palmae	❖ Spring

Palms are fashionable in modern landscape designs, and lend a garden a tropical atmosphere. All palms are easily transplanted and you can have a large palm immediately if you are prepared to pay for it. The bangalow palm, *Archontophoenix cunninghamiana*, is graceful and slender, with a smooth trunk and small cream-to mauve flowers. Alexander palm, *A. alexandrae*, is silver-grey on the undersides of its foliage and grows quickly. It prefers damp conditions and is not as frost tolerant as the bangalow palm.

Many other palms can be grown as specimens or entranceway plants, either in containers or in the ground. Try *Livistona australis* or the kentia palm, *Howea forsteriana*. If palms are out of the question in your area, how about a graceful tree fern?

CEDRELA	◐◑
Chinese toon	▲ To 6 m
Meliaceae	

Deciduous *Cedrela sinensis* is a delightful small tree to grow. In spring its bright pink foliage is outstanding. It fades to a delectable apricot, then cream, and later changes, chameleon-fashion, to green, and finally to lemon in autumn. By gateways or as a specimen tree, the slender *C. sinensis* needs shelter from strong winds and a warm position. Grow it with pink-flowering plants or a blue-flowering ceanothus. Propagate from root cuttings or suckers which you will find round the tree.

CUPRESSUS	◐◑
Cypress	▲ To 6 m
Cupressaceae	

Obelisks on the skyline or sentinels at the gate, upright classical Italian cypress give a Mediterranean look to the garden. The columnar shape combines well with rounded shrubs. *Cupressus sempervirens* 'Stricta' is happy in mild climates, and splendid for gateways. 'Gracilis' is finer, and slower growing. *C. sempervirens* 'Swane's

Golden' is compact, and narrowly columnar. Cypress evoke images of the Riviera and are ideal for the entrances of properties near lakes and by the sea.

MAGNOLIA	◯◗
Magnoliaceae	▲3–15 m
	❖ Spring–summer

Deciduous Chinese magnolias are aristocrats amongst flowering trees, grown and revered for centuries in their native land, portrayed on scrolls and paintings. The Chinese valued plants for their distinctive shape, and their preferred colour was white. *Magnolia denudata* fills these qualifications. Known also as the yulan, this is a magnificent tree, with thick, white, chalice-shaped flowers on bare branches. The blooms are large and sumptuously fragrant. This tree looks fine by wrought-iron or formal wooden gates, or as a specimen tree on a lawn.

M. x. *soulangiana* is a smaller tree but equally pleasant, with shades from white with a hint of pink to deep wine flowers crowding the tips of its bare branches in early spring. M. *campbellii* does not produce its glorious pink flowers for many years. Magnolias are easy to grow in most soils and climates.

Evergreen M. *grandiflora*, from the USA, is another for large entranceways or specimen planting in a lawn. It is, of course, as beautiful as any Chinese species, and its huge flower is gloriously perfumed with overtones of sandalwood and a hint of lemon.

MALUS	◯
Crab apple	▲2.5–6 m
Rosaceae	❖ Spring

The flowering crab apple, *Malus floribunda*, and its hybrids are agreeable specimen trees and good for entranceways. The blossoms smother the well-shaped tree in spring, some being red in bud, opening to a fine pink. The glossy round red crab apples are at their best on varieties such as 'Gorgeous'. Easily grown in rich soil, crab apples are happy in cold conditions. If you can bear to pick the beautiful fruit, it makes excellent jelly.

PRUNUS	◯
Flowering apricot, cherry, peach and plum	▲4–7 m
Rosaceae	❖ Winter–spring

Only poets are able to describe these glorious trees adequately. One of the most popular and best-loved is the weeping cherry, *Prunus subhirtella* 'Pendula' whose dainty blossoms sometimes appear in autumn as well as in early spring. Hybrid forms of *P. serrulata* are also attractive with flowers which range from white to deep rosy-red.

As a specimen tree or by an entranceway, prunus complement most house styles

Flowering cherry

and always enchant. There are dozens of varieties to choose from, with flowers both single and double and in colours from purest white through to dark purple-red. All are hardy in good well-drained soil, but they do not like wind. Cold conditions do not worry prunus.

OTHER TREES AND SHRUBS SUITABLE FOR GATEWAY AND SPECIMEN PLANTINGS

Acacia baileyana — Cootamundra wattle

Acer — maple

Albizia julibrissin — silk tree

Alectryon excelsus — titoki

Backhousia citriodora — lemon ironwood

Betula pendula — silver birch

Callistemon viminalis — weeping bottlebrush

Cedrus — cedar

Chamaecyparis — false cypress

Cornus florida — flowering dogwood

Cotinus — smoke bush

Dacrydium cupressinum — rimu

Eucalyptus ficifolia — red gum

Fraxinus excelsior 'Aurea' — golden ash; *F. raywoodii* — claret ash

Ginkgo — maidenhair tree

Gordonia

Grevillea robusta — silky oak

Hymenosporum — Australian frangipani

Jacaranda

Juniperus chinensis and hybrids

Lagerstroemia — crepe myrtle

Metrosideros kermadecensis 'Variegata' — Kermadec Island pohutukawa

Podocarpus totara — golden totara

Robinia pseudoacacia 'Frisia'

Sophora — kowhai

Viburnum opulus 'Sterile' — snowball tree

OUTDOOR ROOMS

6

Decks, patios and terraces are a link between house and garden — outdoor rooms. They are places for relaxing and should convey a holiday spirit, a feeling of joie de vivre.

Often there is room for al fresco dining here, and decks and patios are great places for entertaining. Such areas should be near a source of music, and in sight and sound of water if possible. For rooms outside you can indulge yourself with exotic planters filled with your favourite shrubs and flowers, fountains, aviaries, special furniture, ornamental lights, wind chimes and wall plaques. The first terrace with container plants was probably in the Hanging Gardens of Babylon, and they were an indulgence if you like.

An archway festooned with a climber can be a most effective entrance. An arch frames a gate, and the view, and provides tantalising glimpses into the garden, rather as a moon gate does.

Traditionally, pergolas are built to provide shade and privacy. Such structures are meant to be clothed with plants, and are most useful to roof a patio or deck, or form part of the entranceway to the house. Sometimes pergolas are built onto the house to meld it with the garden. A free-standing pergola forms an outside room. The frame creates intriguing shadows and it can be built of interesting materials.

Another outside room some gardens feature is the gazebo. A gazebo is essentially a frivolous piece of architecture — a bit of fun and fantasy in the garden. The origin of the word 'gazebo' is hazy, but is thought to come from 'gaze-about'. Originally a gazebo was a two-storied building situated at a vantage point. The first storey contained tools and garden impedimenta, and the upper storey had large windows for gazing-about.

DECKS, PATIOS AND TERRACES

Plants for these outdoor rooms should be selected for their decorativeness and will mostly be at their peak in spring and summer, seasons when outdoor living spaces are in constant use. The scents and night-time appeal of plants should not be forgotten.

Trees and shrubs for growing in containers

Not all patios, decks and terraces can accommodate trees and shrubs. If the deck is on the upper storey of the house, a tree can be planted at ground level to provide privacy and shade. Or a deck may be built around an existing tree to gain the same benefits. Shrubs may be needed for privacy from the street, to provide a screen from neighbours, and for shelter.

We are concerned here with trees and shrubs suitable for growing in containers on the terrace. Many types of containers are now available. Choose these to enhance the style of your surroundings, and in a finish suited to both the colour and shape of the plants they are to contain. If you have several pots on the deck, it is preferable to have them all in the same material and colour. Matching saucers or drip dishes are a good idea. For moving around larger tubs and tree containers, use a small wooden platform fitted with castors.

ACER	◯◑
Japanese maple	▲To 1 m (in pot)
Aceraceae	

New Japanese maples, *Acer palmatum*, are appearing all the time. Many are ideal in containers and have glorious leaf colour. They look very well in large dragon pots. Japanese maples are versatile plants, and fit in to all parts of the ornamental garden. In Europe every palazzo and courtyard seems to have its maple. Such settings are ideal for acers, which cannot tolerate windy positions, but do not mind some shade.

FORTUNELLA	◯
Kumquat	▲1 m
Rutaceae	❖ Winter

Very closely related to citrus species, kumquats are excellent for pot culture. They are prized for their ornamental golden fruits, which can be used in marmalade or in liqueurs. Grow a kumquat in a large wooden tub and surround it with annuals such as pansies, nemesias or primulas. The orange-blossom flowers are intensely fragrant. Kumquats need ample water in summer and citrus manure twice a year. In colder climates remove them to a glasshouse or conservatory during winter.

For a Mediterranean effect, plant this colourful small tree in the classic Versailles tub. These wooden *caisse de Versailles* are exact cubes. A pair of kumquats in two Versailles tubs would look well, especially in conjunction with a striped awning.

FUCHSIA

Onagraceae	▲To 1 m
	❖ Summer–autumn

Fuchsia hybrids do well in containers on shady decks and patios. With hundreds of varieties to choose from, including standard and weeping forms, it is best to go to a specialist for plants. Fuchsias prefer rich soil, ample moisture and filtered light. You must be prepared to water daily and spray the leaves in the heat of summer. Fuchsias are gross feeders and really do best for those who are prepared to give them lots of attention. These plants are fine in pottery containers, wooden tubs and hanging baskets. They do equally well in plastic pots, but do try and disguise these in baskets or other attractive cover-ups. Fuchsias are easily propagated from cuttings taken in autumn or spring.

GARDENIA

Rubiaceae	▲1 m
	❖ All summer

A heavy, seductive scent like no other makes gardenias so special. They are surprisingly easy to grow on a warm patio or deck, requiring only regular watering, and a rich soil with added peat and compost, to stay happy and healthy. Large terracotta or glazed pots suit them well. Try G. *radicans* and G. *jasminoides* 'Florida' for container cultivation.

JUSTICIA

Beloperone; shrimp plant	▲60 cm
Acanthaceae	❖ Year round

Justicia brandegeana flowers continuously in warm districts. Hardy, and not minding soil on the dry side, it is easy to grow in a pot. The flowers are curious, certainly shrimp-shaped, and the colour of cooked shrimp, too, with white-spotted mouths. One cultivar has a pleasing colour combination of lime-green, lemon and white floral bracts. When a plant gets straggly, cut it back; otherwise the shrimp plant needs little attention. It combines well with annuals in a large container, and grows from cuttings.

PODOCARPUS

Buddhist pine	▲2 m (in tub)
Podocarpaceae	

Evergreen *Podocarpus macrophyllus* are stalwart trees, thriving in cooler parts of the patio or deck, and excellent on a formal terrace. Grown in classic wooden Versailles tubs, a line of Buddhist pine looks most elegant, for this variety has a slim, columnar shape, dark green foliage and a patrician air.

Pomegranate	▲ 1 m
Punicaceae	❖ Summer

Pomegranates relish heat and have been grown in the east for centuries. *Punica granatum* 'Nana' is a dwarf version, grown for its brilliant flowers of deep orange to scarlet. Grow in terracotta pots in ordinary potting soil, but feed this shrub regularly. To produce flowers and small fruit, pomegranates need long, hot summers. You can propagate them from seed or cuttings. The foliage is a bonus in autumn, turning richly coloured, and in warm climates the fruit ripens and produces all the seed you will need.

OTHER TREES AND SHRUBS SUITABLE FOR CONTAINERS ON THE DECK, PATIO OR TERRACE

Azalea — evergreen
Boronia
Camellia hybrids (dwarf varieties)
Choisya ternata — Mexican orange blossom
Cistus — rock rose
Citrus — Meyer lemon; Tahitian lime
Convolvulus cneorum
Cordyline australis 'Albertii' — cabbage tree

Hibiscus rosa-sinensis hybrids
Hydrangea
Lantana camara hybrids
Laurus nobilis — bay tree
Meryta — puka
Metrosideros 'Tahiti Red'
Palmae
Pentas
Rhododendron — Vireya
Rosa 'The Fairy'; also the new hybrid patio roses

Climbers for decks and patios

Climbers on decks are frequently grown as screens giving privacy and protection from wind as well as adding beauty to the area. A trellis makes an ideal support. If your deck is on the second storey of the house, a climber such as bougainvillea or honeysuckle can be planted at ground level and encouraged to grow up to the deck and over a trellis or support, perhaps a rail. Other climbers will need to be in containers on the deck itself. Those suitable for growing in containers are marked with an asterisk*. All climbers mentioned are suitable for growing on a trellis.

CALONYCTION*	◑
Moonflower	▲ 1 m in a pot; to 4 m in the ground
Convolvulaceae	❖ Summer

Excellent grown in a pretty pot, the delicate moonflower, *Calonyction aculateum* (now *Ipomoea alba*) is only for a warm terrace. This climber opens its large, white, fragrant flowers with a fanfare. The buds pulsate for up to half an hour before opening in the late afternoon or evening. By morning they are finished, but dozens more will be ready to take over. As you dine on your deck or patio, have a pot

Moonflower

of moonflowers where you can see them as they open, releasing their intoxicating perfume in the night air. Easily grown from seeds in a good potting mix, moonflowers are no trouble to raise. This quick-growing plant is best treated as an annual, and the stems appreciate a support to twine around.

HOYA*	○◑●
Wax plant	▲To 8 m
Asclepiadaceae	❖ Spring–autumn

Hoya carnosa does best in a warm position with plenty of indirect light, on a porch or against a warm and sheltered wall of a deck. Hoyas do not like wind and do best when their roots are contained in a small pot. Partial to a yearly lime drench — use a handful of lime in 8 litres of water — hoyas will give you velvety pink, lightly fragrant flowers faithfully year after year. Do not remove old flowerheads, as the new flowers come from the same stem. Propagate from cuttings.

LONICERA	○◑
Honeysuckle	▲To 6 m
Caprifoliaceae	❖ Spring–summer

Generally the vigorous honeysuckles are best suited for camouflage use or on banks, but *Lonicera sempervirens* is a good evergreen variety to grow up a deck or terrace in a cool climate. It does not mind frost, has pretty red flowers, but alas, no scent. *L. x tellmanniana* has golden-yellow flowers and needs shade. There are also other lonicera hybrids suitable for this purpose.

MANETTIA*	○◐
Rubiaceae	▲2 m
	❖ Year round

Manettia inflata (syn. *M. bicolor*) is a dainty twiner suitable for small decks. Grow it on a trellis in a pot or in the ground. It comes from Brazil and has quaint, two-toned 2 cm flowers in scarlet and gold. It flowers throughout the year, with extra vigour in spring. Propagate by cuttings.

MAURANDIA*	○◐
Scrophulariaceae	▲3 m
	❖ Year round

Maurandia barclaiana (now *Asarina barclaiana*) is another dainty climber with pink, mauve or violet flowers. Maurandias are easily grown from seed, and can be treated as annuals. They germinate so easily you will find plants self-sown round the garden, but they are not invasive. M. *erubescens* and M. *scandens* are others worth cultivating. Maurandias are tolerant of dry conditions and are good growing through other climbers such as bougainvilleas or thunbergias.

OTHER CLIMBERS SUITABLE FOR DECKS, PATIOS OR TERRACES
(Those suitable for growing in containers are marked with an asterisk*)

Asparagus plumosus — asparagus fern*
Bomarea
Bougainvillea*
Clematis species and hybrids
Eccremocarpus — Chilean glory vine*
Hedera — ivy*
Ipomoea 'Heavenly Blue' — morning glory
Jasminum azoricum, J. polyanthum*
Mandevilla 'Alice du Pont'*, M. *sanderi* 'Rosea'*

Mina lobata
Pandorea jasminoides — bower of beauty
Passiflora — passionflower
Pyrostegia — golden shower
Rhodochiton — purple bells*
Solanum jasminoides — potato vine*
Stephanotis — Madagascar jasmine*
Thunbergia*
Trachelospermum jasminoides — Chinese star jasmine

Perennials for pots

Not all perennials are suited to being contained in pots. Only those that are long-lasting in flower, easy to look after and do not grow too large are desirable. Hardy perennials are reliable plants. Look for those pretty in leaf as well as flower.

LEFT: *With a little artful manipulation a lush jungle effect has been produced in a steamy conservatory.*

BELOW: *A delightful room for all-year living, this conservatory provides an airy, light environment for plants.*

*In two different views of the
same garden, grey-leaved
plants thrive in dry conditions.
Here, rosemary and thyme are
used to advantage to team with
other drought-resistant plants
— euphorbias, agapanthus,
and the easy-to-please pepper
tree, Schinus molle.*

EPIDENDRUM ○

Crucifix orchid	▲1 m
Orchidaceae	❖ Year round

One of the easiest orchids to grow is the crucifix orchid, *Epidendrum radicans*, which has tall, cane-like stems and clusters of dainty flowers. Hybrid crucifix orchids flower for months on end in shades of white, palest pink, mauve, yellow, orange, red and wine. Grow them in coarse orchid mix, and water weekly. Crucifix orchids become untidy and leggy unless the old canes are cut back after flowering. They thrive in hanging baskets. Several terracotta pots round the swimming pool featuring epidendrums in different colours look well, too.

GAURA ○

Onagraceae	▲To 1 m
	❖ Summer–autumn

Gaura lindheimeri blooms for a long while and is great for cutting. The small, white butterfly-like flowers are pink in the bud. This ethereal plant looks best in a delicate style of pot. Place it in full sun, for gaura can stand dry conditions, and does not care for being overwatered. Cut back after flowering. It is also fine in beds and borders with its light, lacy look.

IMPATIENS ◐●

Busy Lizzie	▲To 50 cm
Balsaminaceae	❖ Year round

Absolutely out on their own in tubs, troughs, glazed and terracotta pots on decks and patios, double busy Lizzies have flowers as pretty as any rosebud, although sans scent. They are always in flower provided they get generous supplies of water, and occasional fertiliser. In cold districts they are best treated as annuals.

Double impatiens, best for container cultivation, are available in colours from white and palest pink, through all the hot pinks to mauve, orange and red. The New Guinea 'Butterfly' hybrids are an exciting development and produce large, dazzling flowers. You can grow the trouble-free single varieties in pots too; a group of potted single white impatiens on a terrace is most satisfying. The dwarf types are probably at their best in pots when grown as 'fillers' round a shrub.

ORIGANUM ○

Sweet marjoram	▲20 cm
Labiatae	❖ Spring–summer

Invaluable in cooking, *Origanum marjorana* is an attractive herb with soft mauve flowers and fragrant foliage. It is often treated as an annual, being easily propagated from seed and simplicity itself to grow. Sweet marjoram is good in pizza dishes and with tomatoes and seasonings.

Grow this herb with thyme in a trough or terracotta pot on a warm, sunny deck. It will spill over the side of the container most prettily.

PELARGONIUM	○
Geranium	▲50 cm
Geraniaceae	❖ Spring–autumn

Geraniums, as we still insist on calling them, have been much hybridised in Europe and now come in many colours, free flowering, with immense blooms. Easily grown from cuttings, pelargoniums seem to thrive on neglect. They are out on their own on a sunny deck grown in ordinary potting mix. Precocious blooms (from seed to flower in 5 months), the new pelargoniums are worth including in the most sophisticated garden. Hybrids come in multi-colours, from sparkling white to cerise, violet, also bi-coloured and freckled.

STRELITZIA	○
Bird of paradise	▲1–2 m
Musaceae	❖ Winter–spring

Put your *Strelitzia reginae* in a cobalt-blue pot on the deck for a dramatic effect. With a startling colour scheme of orange, yellow and brilliant blue flowerheads, and bold grey-green foliage, strelitzias look impressive, bloom for many months, and are good for cutting. These 'birds of paradise' are easy to grow but need large, straight-sided pots as their root system is dense and massive, and they do not take kindly to being dug up. Get a big plant to begin with, as strelitzias take a while to flower. And they are frost-tender; after all, they are related to bananas. Move them to a sheltered place in winter.

OTHER PERENNIALS SUITABLE FOR GROWING IN POTS ON DECKS, PATIOS OR TERRACES

Campanula — bellflower
Chrysanthemum frutescens
Convolvulus mauritanicus
Diascia
Erigeron karvinskianus —
  babies' tears
Felicia amelloides — blue
  marguerite

Heliotropium — cherry pie;
  heliotrope
Nymphaea — waterlily
Primula — polyanthus
Sedum — stonecrop
Sempervivum tectorum —
  houseleek
Verbena

Container-grown bulbs

It is a good idea to grow your bulbs outside until they are about to flower, then bring them on to the deck or patio where their dazzling display can be best enjoyed. Start your bulbs in a black plastic growing-bag outside, and later transfer bag and all to a waiting pretty pot. Alternatively, plant your bulbs directly into containers and cover with quick-flowering annual seedlings, such as alyssum, dwarf marigolds, forget-me-nots or Virginia stock.

ANEMONE	○
Windflower	▲25 cm
Ranunculaceae	❖ Winter–spring

Anemone coronaria, with flowers as rich and brilliant as in a medieval Book of Hours, arrive in winter to lift our spirits. They are excellent for cutting, and can be bought in separate colours — white, pink, rich velvety purple, blue and brightest crimson. 'De Caen' is the single variety and 'St Brigid' the double. *A. pavonina* 'St. Bravo' strain is strong and sturdy. Anemones appreciate a good, rich, well-drained soil.

HIPPAESTRUM	○
Amaryllidaceae	▲1 m
	❖ Late spring

On a warm terrace in a pot or in the garden, South American hippaestrum hybrids give a dramatic display with their grand trumpet flowers. Plant the large bulb in winter, the neck showing above rich, well-drained potting soil. To give of their best, hippaestrums should be fed weak liquid fertiliser weekly until flowering time.

HYACINTHUS	○
Hyacinth	▲15–25 cm
Liliaceae	❖ Spring

Shallow bowls full of hyacinths are a welcome springtime sight on a deck or terrace. Their fragrance and form is outstanding, and although they prefer cool climates, hyacinths can be persuaded to do well in warm areas in containers. Refrigerate the plump bulbs for a few weeks in autumn before planting, and when you do put them in, make sure the neck of the bulb is at soil level. The popular hardy Dutch hybrids, available in separate, enchanting colours, are the varieties to grow.

LACHENALIA	○
Liliaceae	▲25 cm
	❖ Winter–spring

One of the most cheerful flowers to behold on a chilly winter's day, *Lachenalia aloides* does well on decks. As with most South African bulbs, they prefer a hot, dry summer and a well-drained soil. In a shallow pot or hanging basket they are right for the warm deck and patio. Lachenalias multiply most satisfactorily, and are good for sunny borders and edges in the garden too. Some are bi- and even tri-coloured in red, yellow and green; many of the new hybrids are brilliant. The tubular flowers hang from stiff stems in a most delightful way. Cut back the foliage when it has turned yellow. Start feeding and watering the bulbs again in autumn.

OTHER BULBS SUITABLE FOR GROWING IN CONTAINERS ON DECKS, PATIOS OR TERRACES

Clivia — Kaffir lily	Nerine — spider lily
Freesia	Ranunculus
Muscari — grape hyacinth	Tulipa
Narcissus — daffodil	Zantedeschia — calla lily

Annuals for growing in containers

Annuals provide riotous colour and sheer exuberance to lighten the heart. An inexpensive packet of seed can produce hundreds of plants. Annuals are ideal for pots and many can be used — all you have to do is think of the colour you want and the right position for them. Also see Chapters 2, 8 and 9 for further selection.

BEGONIA	◯◖
Wax begonia	▲15–20 cm
Begoniaceae	❖ Year round

The begonia family is large and has many beautiful members. One of the most versatile and easily grown is *Begonia semperflorens*, a perennial best treated as an annual, which flowers all year and takes no effort to grow from seed in any season except in the coldest districts. Preferring semi-shade, the begonias also enjoy a rich, well-drained soil. You tend to forget them as they just keep on keeping on, demanding little. The colours are white, pink, cream and scarlet to darkest red, with pleasant shiny leaves often in burnished colours.

CAPSICUM	◯
Ornamental chilli	▲30 cm
Solonaceae	❖ Spring–autumn

Capsicum annuum are usually grown for their tasty fruit, but the ornamental variety of chilli are too pretty to pick. On the one plant it is not unusual to get green, cream, yellow, orange and red glossy fruits. The flowers are tiny and insignificant. Terracotta pots and a warm position suit these annuals best.

NEMESIA ○

Scrophulariaceae ▲30 cm

❖ Winter–spring

Nemesias are shallow-rooted and very successful in pots. Their colours are bright and warm just when they are needed with white, cream, yellow, orange, red and even blue blooms over many months ensuring their popularity. Nemesias look well in terracotta pots and wooden tubs. Good drainage and a rich potting mix is necessary. They are easily grown from seed.

OCIMUM ○

Sweet basil ▲35–40 cm

Labiatae ❖ Summer–autumn

Sweet basil, *Ocimum basilicum*, is a most decorative herb. It revels in heat and is most comely with its shiny, aromatic leaves and arching white flowers. Absolutely essential to team with tomatoes, basil will last all the tomato season and beyond. Terracotta pots marry well with this herb, which should preferably be grown on a deck near the kitchen so the cook can make the greatest use of it. Try your hand at making pesto, the scrumptious basil, garlic and pine-nut sauce, an Italian speciality.

PETUNIA ○

Solanaceae ▲30 cm

❖ Spring–autumn

All over the world petunias are a favourite for growing in pots in sunny positions. Single, double, bi-coloured, frilled, veined — there is no end to their diversity. Much hybridised and improved, undemanding petunias are ideal for growing on warm decks, and the colours are a joy. The hotter the summer, the more petunias flower, going on for months on end. Window boxes and hanging baskets also make good homes for petunias. Combine them with white and blue lobelias.

OTHER ANNUALS SUITABLE FOR GROWING IN CONTAINERS ON DECKS, TERRACES AND PATIOS

Ageratum
Bellis perennis — English daisy
Cheiranthus — wallflower
Chrysanthemum — annual
  chrysanthemum
Coleus hybrids
Lobelia
Lobularia — sweet alyssum
Malcomia — Virginia stock

Matthiola — night-scented stock;
  ten-week stock
Phlox drummondii
Primula malacoides — fairy
  primula
Reseda — mignonette
Tagetes — marigolds (French and
  African dwarfs)
Tropaeolum — nasturtium

ARCHWAYS, PERGOLAS AND GAZEBOS

You can train certain boundary hedge plants to form an archway, or use climbers over a support. Roses over an arch are particularly enchanting, and a dainty twiner can be grown with the rose to keep the interest alive throughout the year. Popular climbing roses are listed in Chapter 3, where you will also find many other suitable climbers to clothe the archway and pergola.

Sturdy, more vigorous climbers can be grown over the pergola, whilst the gazebo needs little adornment. A rambling or climbing rose is the traditional decoration, but any of the climbers listed below could enhance your gazebo's appeal.

Climbers for archways, pergolas and gazebos

Climbers beautify these structures. A canopy of shade, a flowery ceiling, a romantic bower — all can be achieved by using the right climbing plants.

PASSIFLORA	○
Passionflower	▲6 m
Passifloraceae	❖ Summer

Several passionflowers are suitable for outside garden rooms. The best, *Passiflora antioquiensis*, is a treasure, with large, pendulous carmine flowers which you need to be underneath to fully appreciate. The egg-shaped edible golden fruits are also most decorative. Mild winters suit them best, and well-drained soil, not over rich. *P. coccinea* is another good one to try in warm areas. Surprisingly, passiflora grow well in quite dry conditions, when they seem to produce the most flowers. The pretty divided leaves stay on the vine all year in most districts. Watch out for the dreaded passion-vine hopper — soapy water sprayed on to the vine retards it.

PYROSTEGIA	○
Golden shower	▲9 m
Bignoniaceae	❖ All winter

Another climber for warm disticts, *Pyrostegia venusta* will romp up and over a fence or a pergola in no time if given well-drained soil and a sunny position. A pergola clothed in orange-gold is a splendid sight in the coldest months of the year, when the great panicles of flowers smother the plant. Pyrostegia will eventually stand a modicum of frost, although when it is young it needs some care.

SOLANUM	◐
Potato vine	▲To 8 m
Solanaceae	❖ Spring–summer

Established plants of *Solanum wendlandii* will withstand drought stoically. The flowers are in glorious Cambridge blue, or sometimes blue-mauve, clusters. This climber looks enchanting growing on a fence or over a pergola or arch. *S. jasminoides*, with its dainty, lacy white flowers and golden anthers, is another for the same structures. Indeed, these two can be grown together.

THUNBERGIA

Acanthaceae ▲3–4 m

❖ Spring–summer

For warm areas only, evergreen *Thunbergia grandiflora* will grow easily, and produce clusters of sky-blue to soft mauve-blue flowers, large, bold and flaring. Its leaves are heart-shaped and deep green. Well-drained soil and a summer mulch is all the attention this climber requires. *T. mysorensis* is entirely different, but just as startlingly beautiful. Long, long racemes hang down in streamers of red, yellow and gold. One for the warmest places, this climber is seen at its best on an archway or pergola, as is the more modest black-eyed Susan, *T. alata*.

WISTERIA

Leguminoseae ▲Up to 20 m

❖ Spring

Wisterias can be trained into standards, encouraged to climb trees, clamber up buildings and cascade over arbours. They are perfect for growing over a pergola, an archway or a gazebo, to give a ravishing umbrella of shade when it is needed. Chinese *Wisteria sinensis* has huge trusses of blue-mauve flowers. The flowers come before the leaves and all summer the foliage provides a fresh green canopy, turning yellow in autumn before falling. Japanese wisteria, *W. floribunda*, has long, dripping trusses of fragrant flowers of a jacaranda blue. *W. floribunda* 'Alba' is a handsome white cultivar, and *W. venusta* is very hardy, with dramatic white flowers.

Wisterias will grow in any good soil, but need sun to flower well. You will need to persuade wisterias on to their support, then prune regularly. Usually the long annual shoots not required are shortened back to about 30 cm in February, and cut back again to within 3 or 4 buds during winter. The best sprays of flowers are formed towards the base of the current year's growth.

OTHER CLIMBERS SUITABLE FOR GROWING OVER ARCHWAYS, PERGOLAS AND GAZEBOS

Actinidia chinensis — kiwifruit (plant male and female for fruit)
Bougainvillea
Campsis — trumpet climber
Clematis montana
Gelsemium — Carolina jasmine
Jasminum azoricum; J. polyanthum
Lonicera hybrids — honeysuckle
Mandevilla laxa — Chilean jasmine

Pandorea jasminoides — bower of beauty
Phaedranthus — Mexican trumpet
Podranea — pink trumpet vine
Rosa — climbing and rambling types
Tecomanthe speciosa
Trachelospermum jasminoides — Chinese star jasmine
Vitis vinifera — grape vine

CONSERVATORIES

7

Trees and shrubs for conservatories • Climbers for conservatories • Annual
climbers for providing shade from outside conservatories • Foliage plants for
conservatories • Flowering plants for conservatories

The conservatory creates an unnatural environment, one which if
left alone would probably be suitable only for growing desert cacti.
Within the conservatory you must exercise a degree of control and
produce a climate sympathetic to your plants. These often need to
be changed round and occasionally taken out of the conservatory
for a break.

In winter you can usually keep the conservatory warm. Summer
is the difficult time, when you must endeavour to make it cooler. Shade
can be provided by appropriate bamboo or fabric blinds; a sun
umbrella will sometimes help. Swathes of calico looped to the ceiling,
paper parasols, rattan screens and shade-cloths all filter the harsh
summer sunlight which damages plants.

A deciduous tree or shrub growing outside the conservatory helps
to keep it cool in summer; inside, a climber will assist, as will an annual
climber on the exterior.

Ventilation is necessary. Ceiling vents can be the answer. People
who are away from home all day do not wish to leave windows open,
and plants must have circulating air. A fan will help.

Plants growing in the conservatory must be watered frequently in
hot weather — indeed, a couple of times a day if you can manage
it — and a mist spray is beneficial. You must keep up the humidity,
and the floor should be tiled or of a material capable of withstanding
the moisture you are going to produce. A spa pool in the conservatory
will help maintain the humidity, or a small ornamental pool.

Plants are beneficial indoors. They rid the air of pollution. It has
been scientifically proven that plants absorb harmful gases and in
return produce oxygen. Romans probably began the practice of
bringing ornamentals inside, so this type of gardening is not new.
The name was conceived and used by John Evelyn in 1664. Originally
a 'conservatory' was a room where plants were 'conserved' in winter.

Trees and shrubs for conservatories

In the conservatory small trees and shrubs are best displayed in attractive containers. Remember you can plant in black plastic growing bags, or plain plastic pots, then put bag or pot temporarily into the container. Most trees and shrubs appreciate a holiday outdoors in the summer.

ALLAMANDA	○
Golden Trumpet	▲ 1–1.5 m
Apocynaceae	❖ Summer

Allamandas are attractive shrubs and climbers from tropical America. *Allamanda cathartica* and its large-flowered cultivar are semi-climbers which bear clusters of golden-yellow trumpets with a dash of apricot inside. These plants like sun and warmth and require a large pot as they can be vigorous growers. As the weather warms, increase the amount of water you give them.

COLLINIA	◑
Parlour palm	▲ To 4 m
Palmae	

Many tropical palms are suited to the conservatory if you are prepared to give them a cool shower in the hot weather. They are excellent by the spa pool. Palms can grow extremely tall and wide — in their natural habitat, some are giants, often reaching over 15 metres. The juvenile forms are the palms we buy. Parlour palm, *Collinia elegans*, is a good choice for a conservatory. As palms appreciate a rest, go easy on the water in cold weather, and be prepared to give them an outdoor holiday in the hottest part of the year. Kentia palm, *Howea forsteriana*, and bamboo palm, *Chamaedorea erumpens*, are also popular.

DRACAENA	◑
Liliaceae	▲ 1.5–3 m

Tall, tropical *Dracaena marginata* is easy to grow in a warm area. The leaves are striped cream or silver and hang lushly in a stunning fountain effect. There are many cultivars. Give dracaenas refreshing sprays in summer, keep the soil moist and do not put them in the sun. They are best suited to a large conservatory.

EUPHORBIA	○
Poinsettia	▲ 50 cm–1.5 m
Euphorbiaceae	❖ Winter–spring

Your poinsettia, *Euphorbia pulcherrima*, will not want to spend all year in the conservatory, but when its flowerheads are developing, bring it inside and water faithfully. Winter temperatures should be no lower than 13°C. The bracts come in colours of cream and pink as well as the favourite fire-engine red. For house plants, poinsettias are chemically dwarfed; after a year or two they will start growing large. In warm areas plant them outside in the garden. Give poinsettias good light and some sun, but note that they need 12 hours of darkness each day before they will deign to flower.

FICUS	◑
Weeping fig	▲1.5–2 m
Moraceae	

Weeping fig, *Ficus benjamina*, likes a humid, warm place. Coming from India, it needs temperatures between 13–20°C in winter and spring. The weeping fig appreciates water on its leaves. Spray frequently in summer, or carry it into your bathroom and give it a gentle shower. During the rest of the year the weeping fig does not require more than a weekly watering. Underpot, and watch out for mealy bugs and maybe scale insects. Fiddle-leaf fig, *F. lyrata*, can be treated in a similar fashion, as can the rubber tree, *F. elastica*.

PLUMERIA	○
Frangipani	▲1–2 m
Apocynaceae	❖ Summer–autumn

Frangipani is a reminder of welcoming leis in Hawaii and South Pacific Islands. It grows beautifully in a warm conservatory in a tub. Give it a well-drained potting mix, and copious summer watering to stimulate flower growth, for in its natural habitat frangipani gets bounteous summer rain. A powerfully seductive scent is a large part of the frangipani's attraction. The easiest to grow is the cream-flowering *Plumeria acutifolia*.

Frangipani

Fortunella — kumquat
Gardenia
Heimerliodendron — parapara
Hibiscus rosa-sinensis hybrids
Ixora

Justicia — lobster plant
Punica — dwarf pomegranate
Schefflera (syn. Brassaia) —
    umbrella tree
Streptosolen — marmalade bush

Climbers for conservatories

To provide shade for the conservatory, as well as colour at eye level and above, it is practicable to grow a climber. A perennial climber for your indoor garden will need to be chosen with great care, as it will be a permanent fixture, too difficult to move about. For shade in summer, you can also grow an annual climber outside the conservatory.

CISSUS ○◗

Kangaroo vine ▲4 m

Vitaceae

Australian kangaroo vine, *Cissus antarctica*, climbs well, and is content in a container of potting mix. It will help shade the conservatory from the sun. *C. antarctica* needs watering and feeding throughout summer. *C. discolor* from South-east Asia requires more winter warmth and humidity. All cissus species are grown for their bold, handsome leaves.

CLERODENDRUM ○

Clerodendron ▲Up to 4 m

Verbenaceae ❖ Spring–summer

Clerodendrum thomsoniae bears clusters of white calyces and flaring, brilliant red flowers flying from them in a most unusual way. *C. splendens* has crimson flowers in clusters. Both are easy to maintain, and can be planted in an ordinary potting mix. They need warmth, lots of light and plenty of water in the growing season.

IPOMOEA ○

Cardinal creeper ▲Up to 5 m

Convolvulaceae ❖ All year

Cardinal creeper, *Ipomoea horsfalliae*, is a quick-growing perennial climber which relishes heat. Grow it in potting mix enriched with loam and leaf mould. This ipomoea is bedecked with carmine flowers amongst its bright green leaves at all times of the year.

RHAPHIDOPHORA ○

Araceae ▲2 m

Rhaphidophora aurea (syn. *Scindapsus aurea*) will grow easily up a bamboo pole or in a hanging basket. It is vigorous and rampant and will climb all over the conservatory, given half a chance. In winter *R. aurea* will appreciate warmth and indirect light to retain leaf colour. It reproduces with great ease — simply break off a piece and start again.

STEPHANOTIS ○

Madagascar vine ▲3–4 m

Asclepiadaceae ❖ Summer

Sumptuously scented *Stephanotis floribunda* has waxy clusters of pure white tubular flowers which are much used for wedding bouquets. Ordinary potting mix will be quite acceptable to this climber, and it needs a generous pot. Mealy bug can trouble it. Stephanotis has tough, leathery leaves and is not at all delicate in conservatories, or out in the open in warmer districts. Water well in summer and feed occasionally.

OTHER CLIMBERS SUITABLE FOR GROWING IN CONSERVATORIES

Aloe ciliaris — climbing aloe
Bougainvillea
Calonyction — moonflower
Gloriosa — glory lily
Hoya — wax plant

Pereskia — lemon vine; Barbados
  gooseberry
Philodendron
Thunbergia alata — black-eyed
  Susan

Annual climbers for providing shade from outside conservatories

Transient annual climbers, or perennials best treated as annuals, are good to grow against the outside of the conservatory to provide shade when it is needed most. All recommended are easily grown from seed.

COBAEA ○◗

Cathedral bells ▲3 m

Polemoniaceae ❖ Year round

Cobaea scandens is a good Mexican perennial climber. Usually treated as an annual, it is ridiculously easy to grow from seed. The large, cup-shaped flowers are produced prolifically, and are soft lime green, deepening to mauve and then purple.

IPOMOEA	◯
Morning glory	▲2 m
Convolvulaceae	❖ Summer–autumn

Ipomoea tricolor 'Heavenly Blue' is a perennial best treated as an annual and easily grown from seed, in a warm, wind-free position. Very precocious, it will cover a fence or wall in a few months and produce flowers of translucent, heavenly blue. Looks good on an archway, too, and is ideal against the conservatory.

LATHYRUS	◯
Sweet pea	▲To 3 m
Leguminosae	❖ Spring–summer

Most gardeners have grown annual sweet peas at some time. Just right against a sunny fence or wall facing north, provided some support is given, sweet peas prefer the soil to be prepared ahead with potash and lime. It must be well-drained and friable. Sweet peas should be picked regularly to ensure continuous flowering. This is no hardship as sweet peas are among the prettiest cut flowers and their perfume will scent a room delightfully.

MINA	◯
Convolvulaceae	▲2 m
	❖ Summer–autumn

The old-fashioned climber *Mina lobata*, another perennial best treated as an annual, has had a facelift and is in a much improved form now, bearing spectacular flowers of red, orange, yellow and white. Each seed seems to germinate, and thousands of flowers are produced on just a few plants. Grow *M. lobata* behind plants with autumn tonings.

RHODOCHITON	◯
Purple bells	▲2 m
Scrophulariaceae	❖ Summer–autumn

A twining, fastidious plant with parasol-shaped fuchsia calyces from which emerge purple corollas, *Rhodochiton atrosanguineum* is easily grown inside or out. Although a perennial, it is best treated as an annual and is easily propagated from seed. The plants are precocious, their purple bells flowering in 3–4 months from sowing.

Foliage plants for conservatories

To give the conservatory a tropical appearance, plants with brilliant leaves and large, 'architectural' foliage fit the bill. To grow such plants in a tropical atmosphere, high humidity is essential, although less needed in winter. Alternatively, you might decide to settle for a desert environment; if so, try cactus in brilliantly decorated terracotta pots, Mexican fashion. Some succulents, with their fascinating textures, are also happy in a dry environment. The amazing crassula family survive in droughts and seem to positively enjoy fasting.

ASPLENIUM	◑●
Hen-and-chicken fern; bird's-nest fern	▲To 1 m
Aspleniaceae	

Aspleniums are a diverse species, available in a wide variety of shapes and sizes. *Asplenium bulbiferum*, the quickly multiplying hen-and-chicken fern, is easy to grow outside or in, and must have shade, as must all ferns. Bird's-nest fern, *A. nidus-avis*, has shiny, bright-green bold leaves and does very well indoors. Place it on the floor for maximum effect.

Ferns are suited to bathrooms and spa rooms, and in the summer you could move them to here from the conservatory. Grow in leaf mould and a peaty potting mix. Spray the foliage on hot days, and keep ferns right away from sun.

CALADIUM	◐
Araceae	▲30–40 cm

Caladium cultivars have bold, arrow-shaped leaves of dazzling, clashing colours — nothing could be more tropical looking. Caladiums must have heat, humidity and moisture. Stand their pots in a tray of damp pebbles and keep out of direct sunlight, but in the light. They respond to regular feeding. Some have heavily veined leaves of green, white, red and chocolate, others white with green or pink with green.

Caladiums are dormant in the winter. Gradually stop their watering and leave them in a warm dry place till spring, then replant the tuberous rhizomes in rich loam and compost and keep them shaded from strong sunlight. Mist spray daily. It must be admitted caladiums are difficult plants, but very rewarding if kept happy.

CODIAEUM	○
Croton	▲To 1 m
Euphorbiaceae	❖ Spring–summer

Just to look at crotons, *Codiaeum pictum*, is to be reminded of the tropics. The bold leaves splashed with greens, yellow, copper and brilliant red appear the essence of heat and sun. Crotons need bright, filtered light, ample moisture and humidity. In the hottest summer weather, take them outside for a holiday. Propagate from cuttings and grow in a well-drained potting mix with peat. Many different varieties and cultivars are available. Grow several together for impact, and with other plants too.

NEPHROLEPIS

Boston fern ▲To 1 m

Oleandraceae

The most popular houseplants, Boston fern, *Nephrolepis exaltata*, has lengthy fronds and is best in hanging baskets or large pots. Originally from tropical regions, nephrolepis do not care for draughts and bright sunlight. Spray with water during the hot weather and watch out for scale insects. Keep the humidity high and be prepared to move them in the summer to a cooler but well-lit part of the house.

OTHER FOLIAGE PLANTS SUITABLE FOR CONSERVATORIES

Alocasià — elephant's ear	Echevaria
Begonia — leaf types	Monstera — fruit-salad plant
Calathea — peacock plant	Peperomia
Chlorophytum — spider plant	Pilea — aluminium plant
Coleus hybrids	Sansevieria — mother-in-law's-
Cordyline terminalis — ti	tongue
Crassula	Sedum
Ctenanthe — never-never plant	*Tillandsia usneioides* — Spanish
Dieffenbachia — dumb cane	moss

Flowering plants for conservatories

Flowering plants will provide gaiety and cheerfulness in the conservatory. Pot up annuals for winter colour. Use those described in Chapter 6 on decks and patios (p. 84–5). Also bring inside orchid cactus, the epiphyllums, in spring, and tuberous begonias, and cyclamen in winter. Cymbidium orchids, which are better off outdoors all summer, can be displayed in the conservatory during their winter flowering season.

ANTHURIUM ◑

Flamingo flower ▲To 80 cm

Araceae ❖Year round

Anthurium blooms have shiny, brilliant red spathes, as though lacquered. The hybrids come in various other startling colours. Of the numerous anthuriums available, most are cultivated for their long-lasting flowers, but *A. warocqueanum* is grown for its splendid velvety, deep green leaves, which are smartly veined in lime green. Moisture and humidity is needed, indirect sunlight, and a temperature not less than 10°C in winter. Great plants for the indoor spa room, relishing the warm, humid atmosphere, anthuriums create a tropical ambience like few other plants.

LEFT: *Tough pampas grass is an attractive choice for an exposed site.*

BELOW: *A colourful garden, overlooking a sheltered bay, makes the most of a benign climate, and utilises shells from the beach for paths.*

TOP RIGHT: Eastern calm is conveyed by an oriental bridge spanning a tranquil pool.

RIGHT: Hostas and bog primulas relish damp conditions at the water's edge.

BELOW: Cool green reflections in a formal pool can be viewed from the house.

EUCHARIS ◑

| Amazon lily | ▲90 cm |
| Amaryllidaceae | ❖ Summer |

You must have a large pot for *Eucharis amazonica*, and do stand it in the almost obligatory tray of pebbles to gain enough humidity. It will not tolerate any temperatures below 13°C in the winter. The flowers resemble crystal-white daffodils and are deliciously fragrant. On long stems, each one with 3 to 6 flowers, the Amazon lily never fails to delight. Propagate from offsets and grow in potting mix with extra leaf mould.

LAELIA ◯◑

| Orchidaceae | ▲50 cm |
| | ❖ Autumn–winter |

Orchids are a large, complex family with differing needs. *Laelia anceps* is an easy orchid for beginners to cultivate, though it needs more heat than the cymbidium. Pot in orchid mix, grow outside in the shadehouse for the summer and then bring inside as the flowerbuds form. The flowers are enchanting, being clear mauve with a velvety, deep-purple lip.

SINNINGIA ◯◑

| Gloxinia | ▲25 cm |
| Gesneraceae | ❖ All summer |

A summer-flowering hothouse plant which blooms in colours rich and royal, as beautiful and glowing as a page from a medieval Book of Hours, gloxinia, *Sinningia speciosa*, can be tricky. Pot up in early spring in peat and humus-laden potting mix, keep consistently moist, be generous with liquid fertiliser and put in a bright light. When the flowers have faded, reduce watering and store, pot and all, in a cool, dark, dry place over winter.

OTHER PLANTS WITH FLOWERS SUITABLE FOR CONSERVATORIES

Acalypha 'Summer Love'
Aphelandra — zebra plant
Calceolaria
Capsicum annum — ornamental chilli
Columnea
Dionaea — Venus fly-trap
Episcia
Heliconia psittacorum — parrot flower
Hoya bella — wax plant
Kalanchoe
Medinilla magnifica
Nopalxochia — orchid cactus
Schlumbergera — crab cactus; Christmas cactus
Sempervivum — houseleek
Streptocarpus hybrids
Vriesia psittacina — bromeliad

DRY-CLIMATE GARDENS

8

Trees and shrubs for dry conditions • Climbers for dry conditions • Perennials for dry conditions • Bulbs for dry conditions • Annuals for dry conditions

---

Dry-climate gardening is a challenge. As a rule, plants must endure extremes of climate in dry areas. Varieties hardy to drought are essential here, for dry-climate gardeners cannot always afford the luxury of watering the garden. If water is available, it is best to soak the plants once a week, rather than giving them a superficial sprinkling every day or so.

Mulching is desirable in any garden, essential in a dry one. Mulch reduces evaporation and so conserves soil moisture. It prevents damage to the soil structure and improves texture and condition. Garden compost, mushroom compost, bark chips, straw, grass clippings and sawdust are all good mulches. These organic mulches should not be used fresh, as they will take nutrients out of the soil. If you are forced to use fresh materials, apply a nitrogenous fertiliser as well, but it is always preferable to use well-rotted mulch, in thin layers.

In areas of dry climate, establish plants in autumn so they get a good start, and make sure they do not have to compete with strong perennial weeds. Use tough species native to dry areas, and do select the appropriate fruit trees — apricots and almonds do well in hot, dry inland areas, and figs are superb here.

Trees and shrubs for dry conditions

Extra care at planting time is essential for shrubs and trees having to endure dry conditions. Incorporate humus in the planting hole and a handful of damp peat. Mulching, of course, is necessary, and a good plan is to place rocks round trees and shrubs as you stake them, to help secure them and to keep roots cool — hot, dry winds wreak havoc with newly planted shrubs. Autumn planting is preferable, to give plants a good start.

Many Southern Hemisphere native trees and shrubs have the ability to survive in adverse conditions, and the tough coastal trees likewise. The shrubs of the dry, stony *maquis* of Mediterranean regions — lavender, genista, rosemary, cistus and junipers — are of course logical varieties for growing in any dry climate.

AGONIS	◯◑
Willow myrtle	▲3–6 m
Myrtaceae	❖ Winter–spring

Agonis flexuosa from Western Australia is hardy and drought resistant, as indeed are all the agonis species. A slender, drooping, graceful tree, the willow myrtle produces pretty, white, long-lasting blooms. It does better when pruned back after flowering. A bonus with all the species, the agonis flowers are easily dried for everlastings. They tolerate mild but not severe frosts.

ALBIZIA	◯
Silk tree	▲To 4 m
Leguminosae	❖ Summer

The silk tree, *Albizia julibrissin*, is pretty in leaf and flower. Tufts of silky pink flowers top the spreading small deciduous tree. It is best to have it growing where you can look down upon it. The ferny foliage closes at night. The silk tree makes a fine specimen tree — it is not leafless for long and is graceful in growth. Other albizias are at home in dry conditions but are not nearly as comely.

EUCALYPTUS	◯
Gum tree	▲To 6 m
Myrtaceae	❖ Winter–summer

Small-growing eucalypts are best for smaller gardens. Red gum, *Eucalyptus ficifolia*, is deservedly popular with its bright-red flowers. In areas of low humidity all the western eucalypts are the varieties to plant. *E. caesia* is handsome, with weeping grey leaves and pink to red flowers. Another with grey foliage is *E. rhodantha*. Propagate from seed.

LEUCOSPERMUM ○

Proteaceae ▲ 1–2.5 m

❖ Spring

The South African leucospermums are admirable shrubs. It is difficult to short-list the best: perhaps *Leucospermum cordifolium*, with apricot, fat, rounded pincushions, or *L. reflexum*, with its attractive grey foliage and tangerine to red flowers, or yellow-flowered *L. reflexum* var. *luteum*. Hardy *L. conocarpodendron* has butter-yellow blooms. Do not attempt leucospermums if your soil contains lime, or if the area is subject to heavy frosts.

MELIA ○

Indian bead tree ▲ 3 m

Meliaceae ❖ Spring

In many towns in warm, dry, areas the Indian bead tree, *Melia azedarach*, reigns supreme as a street tree. It is neat and airy, with sweet lilac flowers, followed by round yellow berries. This tree grows quickly and easily.

OLEA ○

Olive ▲ 3 m

Oleaceae ❖ Spring

The olive, *Olea purpurea*, has been grown in the Mediterranean since the earliest times. Pliny the Elder wrote: 'There are two liquids pleasing to the body, inwardly wine and outwardly oil, and they both come from trees'. He was right about the oil anyway. Olive trees are evocative of the countryside of Southern Europe and the Mediterranean. Old, twisted olive trees with lavender growing under and round them are a feature of southern Italy. Grow olives in a grove if you can, or as a specimen underplanted with grey-leaved or blue-flowering plants to create a cool oasis. You can harvest the olives if the birds will let you. When the wind ruffles the leaves of the olive, they glisten silver and mother-of-pearl — a lovely sight.

ROBINIA ○

Leguminosae ▲ To 8 m

❖ Spring

Deciduous robinias are very hardy. Some species make fine specimen trees and are able to withstand hot, dry winds and extreme temperatures. *Robinia pseudoacacia* 'Frisia' is the popular variety with glowing luminous foliage of golden lime, retained from spring to autumn. 'Frisia' has small, fragrant cream flowers. The pink wisteria tree, *R. decaisneana*, is a quick-growing medium-sized tree, neat in shape and bearing cascades of scented shell-pink flowers. *R. floreyi* has white blooms.

OTHER TREES AND SHRUBS SUITABLE FOR DRY CONDITIONS

Acacia — wattle
Arbutus unedo — Irish strawberry
   tree
Banksia
Berberis — barberry
Brachychiton acerifolius —
   Illawarra flame tree
Buddleia salvifolia — butterfly bush
Callistemon — bottlebrush
Ceanothus — Californian lilac
Cercis — Judas tree
Cistus — rock rose
Cotinus — smoke bush
Crotalaria — bird flower
Cytisus — broom
Dryandra
Echium
Erica
Euphorbia
Euyrops
Fremontodendron — fremontia
Genista — broom
Gleditsia — honey locust
Juniperus

Koelreuteria — golden rain tree
Lagunaria — Norfolk Is. hibiscus
Lantana camara hybrids;
   L. montevidensis
Lavandula
Leucadendron
Mahonia
Melaleuca
Myoporum — ngaio
Nerium — oleander
Phoenix — phoenix palm
Pinus
Pistacia — pistachio
Podalyria calyptrata — sweet pea
   bush; *P. sericea* — satin bush
Protea
Rhaphiolepis — Indian hawthorn
Rosmarinus — rosemary
Santolina — lavender cotton
Schinus molle — pepper tree
Spartium — Spanish broom
Tamarix
Virgilia
Westringia — coast rosemary

Climbers for dry conditions

Many climbers will grow well in dry conditions, but most do not care for open, windy positions. Remember to mulch them in the summer, and secure them well.

CAMPSIS	○
Trumpet climber	▲To 5 m
Bignoniaceae	❖ Summer–autumn

Stalwart deciduous climbers, campsis will grow well in low-rainfall areas provided they get hot summers. The best known is *Campsis* x *tagliabuana* 'Madam Galen', which has typical terracotta to Titian-red trumpets. *C. grandiflora* from China has flowers about 7 cm long, often apricot, sometimes red in colour. *C. radicans* will stand very cold winters. Often grown on fences or against walls, all campsis are robust and pretty tough. They are easily propagated by cuttings and suckers.

GLORIOSA	○◗
Glory lily	▲2–4 m
Liliaceae	❖ Summer

Often grown in pots, the dainty *Gloriosa rothschildiana* is native to East Africa and needs heat. The flowers, crimson and gold, are curved back, and the large stamens swing down. G. *superba* is hardier and not quite as entrancing. It grows wild in Zimbabwe and South Africa. Grown from tubers, gloriosa die down immediately after flowering. Light soil suits them, and they will stand light frosts as they are dormant in winter.

HARDENBERGIA	◯◑
False sarsaparilla	▲1.5–3 m
Leguminosae	❖ Winter–spring

At home in dry and coastal gardens, *Hardenbergia violacea* is a hardy, evergreen, bushy climber producing small pea-like flowers which cover the entire plant. The flowers vary in colour, purple being most common, but white and pink varieties exist. This vine is versatile and can be used as a groundcover, or to cascade down a bank. *H. comptoniana* is similar and just as easy to grow. The flowers are in sprays of lilac. Hardenbergias will thrive in all but the coldest climates in most soils, and are propagated from hardwood cuttings.

PODRANEA	◯
Pink trumpet vine	▲To 9 m
Bignoniaceae	❖ Summer–autumn

A rampant climber once it gets going, *Podranea ricasoliana* requires a big garden to do it justice. It looks impressive with its bold pink trumpets when grown through a large tree. In cold climates this Zimbabwe creeper loses its leaves in winter. Propagated by layering or cuttings, it excels in the dry garden in all soil types.

ROSA	◯◑
Rambling and climbing roses	▲To 10 m
Rosaceae	❖ Spring–summer

Climbing and rambling roses are suited to many places in the garden, and some grow admirably in dry, arid areas. The bonny, versatile *Rosa* 'Climbing Iceberg' will do well here. The rambler roses are much hybridised; many derive from the ultra-hardy *R. wichuraiana*, and some are good for ground covering. Banksia rose, *R. banksiae lutea*, will do well in dry situations. *R. rugosa* 'Alba' will grow in dry sand dunes, and its comely single flowers are followed by large fruits. Other suitable climbing and rambling roses are described in Chapter 1.

TRACHELOSPERMUM	◯◑
Chinese star jasmine	▲5 m
Apocynaceae	❖ Late spring–summer

This lovely evergreen climber has flowers with a fragrance unrivalled by any manufactured scent. *Trachelospermum jasminoides* grows well on a pergola, trellis or as a groundcover on a bank, and it will tolerate extremes of climate. Altogether a delightful climber, the Chinese star jasmine has no vices, and pests and diseases leave it alone. It can be increased by cuttings.

OTHER CLIMBERS SUITABLE FOR DRY CONDITIONS

Akebia quinata	*Macfadyena unguis-cati* (syn.
Bougainvillea	*Doxantha unguis-cati*) cat's paw
Ficus pumila — creeping fig	Pelargonium — climbing geranium,
Hedera — ivy	ivy-leaved geranium
Kennedia — coral pea	*Thunbergia alata* — black-eyed
Lonicera — honeysuckle	Susan

Perennials for dry conditions

Perennials on the whole prefer less harsh conditions than dry gardens can provide. However, if you are prepared to cosset them, perennials can be very rewarding here. Many perennials suited to the coast (see Chapter 9) also grow adequately in arid areas. Perennials with grey and silver leaves, and many of the succulents, will thrive. Some shade-loving perennials will also prosper, provided they have mulch and extra attention. (See Chapter 11 for suitable varieties.) Mix wetted peat with the soil when you plant such perennials.

Generally perennials are more labour-intensive than shrubs to grow successfully in dry areas. Merge with bulbs and mingle with protective, hardy shrubs.

ACHILLEA	○
Yarrow	▲45–60 cm
Compositae	❖ Summer

This large genus contains many species, mostly without enemies and all ultra-hardy. *Achillea filipendulina* has heads of yellow to mustard flowers combined with ferny foliage. *A. millefolium* hybrids have flowers in pretty pastels, award winners. Look for 'Summer Pastels'. *A. ptarmica* 'The Pearl', an old favourite with white double and semi-double blooms, is a fine groundcover. All achilleas are good for cutting and drying, and for growing in English meadow gardens. (See Chapter 12.)

FELICIA	○
Blue marguerite	▲45 cm
Compositae	❖ Nearly all year

From South Africa, *Felicia amelloides* is drought resistant and has golden-eyed daisies of an intense blue. Be generous with it — grow blue marguerites in clumps, in drifts, near yellow and white flowering plants. Try the variegated foliage version. Bushy blue marguerites, with their almost constant supply of flowers, complement many other plants. They are easily propagated by cuttings, and look well in containers too.

NEPETA	○
Catmint	▲ To 70 cm
Labiatae	❖ Summer

Cats are partial to all the catmint species, and it is the aromatic silver-grey foliage which attracts them. The catmints are good groundcovers and will spread obligingly amongst their neighbours in the dry garden. *Nepeta* x *faassenii* has spires of lavender-blue flowers. You can make catmint 'mice' and 'pussy pillows' from the dried leaves, as gifts to spoilt cats. Prune catmints back after flowering and propagate from cuttings.

ROMNEYA	○
Californian 'tree' poppy; Matilija poppy	▲ 1–1.8 m
Papaveraceae	❖ Summer

Immense, pure-white, papery flowers bedeck *Romneya coulteri*, which grow large and will spread — they resent disturbance. The attractive glaucous leaves appear in late winter, before the especially beautiful bold flowers with their gold stamens, which are good for picking. Gravelly soil suits them.

YUCCA	○
Agavaceae	▲ 2.5 m
	❖ Spring–autumn

Yucca filamentosa has large, erect panicles of creamy-coloured flowers. Bold and tropical-looking, yuccas are drought resistant and come from desert areas. Unfortunately the ends of the pointed leaves are razor sharp and so this plant should not be grown right by a path. Propagate from seed, and give yuccas plenty of room.

OTHER PERENNIALS SUITABLE FOR DRY CONDITIONS

Agapanthus
Anthemis cupaniana
Arctotis — African daisy
Artemisia
Aubrieta
Bergenia
Campanula isophylla — Italian bellflower
Centranthus — valerian
Crassula
Echevaria

Eryngium — sea holly
Euphorbia
Gaura
Gazania — treasure flower
Helianthemum — rock rose
Helichrysum italicum
Iberis sempervirens — perennial candytuft
Salvia
Sedum — stonecrop
Sempervivum — houseleek

Bulbs for dry conditions

Happily, many South African bulbs revel in dry conditions. The summer-flowering bulbs are usually the best, i.e. those having hard corms.

BABIANA	○
Baboon flower	▲25 cm
Iridaceae	❖ Spring

Babiana stricta, from Africa, has naturalised in hot, dry areas in many countries. Baboons purportedly dig up and eat the bulbs. Do not emulate them — they taste awful. Babianas do need some water in winter, and at flowering time. Blooms range in shades from blue to purple, occasionally white; some are rather harsh in colour. Babianas increase with the greatest of ease.

IXIA	○
Iridaceae	▲45 cm
	❖ Spring–early summer

Ixias flourish almost anywhere, unless the winters are exceptionally cold. *Ixia maculata* has flowers of pink, cerise and cream. *I. viridiflora* is the one with the amazing turquoise flowers. Ixias naturalise easily, and increase at a great rate.

Ixia

NERINE	$\bigcirc\!\!\!\!\!\bullet$
Spider lily	▲To 60 cm
Amaryllidaceae	❖ Late summer–autumn

If you have room for only one type of bulb in the dry garden, make it nerines. They start flowering when the garden is decidedly middle-aged, and their fresh- ness and colour rejuvenates any tired border. *Nerine fothergillii* 'Major' is a bold scarlet and has many hybrids in colours from white to red. Pink *N. bowdenii* is tough and will take frosts, unlike the other species. Guernsey lily, *N. sarniensis*, has scarlet iridescent flowers sprinkled with gold dust. *N. sarniensis* 'Virgo' is a charming white. All are long lasting as cut flowers. Most will grow under trees, tolerating light shade.

ROMULEA	$\bigcirc$
Iridaceae	▲10–15 cm
	❖ Winter–spring

Romuleas are hardy to frost, and are easily grown, but must have full sun to flower. Pretty wee things, suitable for edges, banks and shallow containers, romuleas flower with great gusto. *Romulea sabulosa* has surprisingly large flowers for its size, coloured a shiny ruby red with deep-green to purple inner portions. Other species are also worthwhile growing, the flowers coming in shades of blue, yellow and pink. All species grow easily from seed.

TRITONIA	$\bigcirc$
Iridaceae	▲30–45 cm
	❖ Late spring–summer

Yet another South African, and hardy with it, tritonias provide flower continuity in the bulb bed. *Tritonia crocata* is the most useful, with its surprising orange blooms. Other forms have flowers of white, salmon and scarlet, all on short, wiry stems. Usually grown in borders or mixed with sparaxis, which they resemble, tritonias multiply easily and will naturalise in grass.

OTHER BULBS SUITABLE FOR DRY CONDITIONS

Allium — ornamental onion
Amaryllis — belladonna lily
Freesia
Lachenalia

Lycoris — spider lily
Sandersonia
Sparaxis
Tulipa
Watsonia — bugle lily

Annuals for dry conditions

In dry gardens annuals are a valuable part of the design. When droughts are a concern, hardy annuals provide quick replacements and useful ground cover around more permanent plants.

AMARANTHUS	○
Joseph's coat; love-lies-bleeding	▲To 1 m
Amaranthaceae	❖ Summer

Amaranthus are an interesting genus, some South American species being valuable food sources, but love-lies-bleeding, *Amaranthus caudatus*, is appreciated for its tassel-like crimson flowers. There is also a green variety. Joseph's coat, *A. tricolor*, lives up to its name, with leaves brightly coloured in shades of red, tan, .bronze, and some yellow and green. Amaranthus appreciate heat and will colour best in poor soil. They are easily and quickly grown from seed.

CELOSIA	○
Cockscomb; Prince of Wales feather	▲70 cm
Amaranthaceae	❖ Summer

Crested heads of fiery reds, golds, orange and yellow are the hallmark of *Celosia plumosa*. The peculiar cockscomb, *C. cristata* has velvety, convoluted flowers, in autumnal colours. Celosia is easily grown from seed.

DIMORPOTHECA	○
Star of the veldt	▲25 cm
Compositae	❖ Summer–autumn

Bearing pretty daisies in unusual colours, in pastel shades of salmon, apricot, pink and lemon, star of the veldt has only one fault — the flowers close in shady weather. Much hybridised, dimorpotheca are covered in blooms for a long period of the year. These plants look well in a border, or in containers, and amongst summer-flowering bulbs. Very versatile, they are easily grown from seed.

ECHIUM	○
Boraginaceae	▲50–90 cm
	❖ Summer

Echium lycopsis and hybrids have showy spikes of pink, white, blue and mauve flowers. Easy to grow from seed, these echiums look best in drifts or clumps in the dry garden, and will not be invasive.

GLAUCIUM	○
Horned poppy	▲To 45 cm
Papaveraceae	❖ All summer

Excellent for light, sandy soils, on the coast as well as inland, glaucium species are all worth growing. Their colours range in warm shades: scarlet, orange and gold. You need to grow a good many together for a brilliant show, but horned poppies propagate easily from seed, so mass plantings are not hard to achieve.

TAGETES	○
French and African marigolds	▲To 60 cm
Compositae	❖ Summer–winter

Despite their common names, tagetes really hale from Mexico. They flower profusely over a long season, coming in colours of bright yellow, orange, tan and Titian red. Pale colours of white, cream and lemon are also now appearing. The current trend is to breed them short and stocky, with large flowers. Tiny *Tagetes signata* is suitable for pots and edging. All are ridiculously easy to grow from seed. Place the rather raucous shades amongst more sober perennials and annuals.

OTHER ANNUALS SUITABLE FOR DRY CONDITIONS

Cleome — spider flower
Craspedia globosa — billy buttons
Eschscholzia — California poppy
Gomphrena — globe everlasting
Helipterum — paper daisy
Limonium — statice
Linum — annual flax

Lonas annua
Mesembryanthemum — Livingstone daisy
Petunia
Portulaca
Tropaeolum — nasturtium

SEASIDE GARDENS

9

Trees and shrubs for seaside gardens • Climbers for seaside gardens • Perennials for seaside gardens • Bulbs for seaside gardens • Annuals for seaside gardens

---

Living by the sea has many advantages. However, it is not quite paradise for gardeners. Often the soil is downright poor, either dry and sandy, or hard, unyielding clay. Salty sea breezes, and sometimes gales, have to be contended with, in often fickle climates. Yet, with shelter, seaside plantings can be as lush as any other, and if they have a backdrop of the sea, coastal gardens are breathtakingly beautiful. Many Australian native plants thrive by the sea, and a number of these will withstand the worst conditions.

One great advantage of coastal gardens is that generally they are frost free. Another asset is the seaweed gathered from the beach, useful for much-needed humus. And not all seaside gardens are severely exposed to hostile elements. There are many warm sheltered bays.

Trees and shrubs for seaside gardens

Trees and shrubs are the first line of defence from fierce, salty winds. They in turn help cosset more tender plants. Shrubs and trees which are quick-growing and able to put up with spray and exposed situations are marked with an asterisk* in the list below. They act as nursemaids. After they have formed secure shelter from winds, you can introduce other shrubs into the seaside garden.

Great care is needed when planting trees and shrubs at the coast. Make sure they are securely staked and mulched — a heavy stone or rock at the base will help, and a temporary brush shelter will protect them. After a gale, give young trees and shrubs a hosing down to remove damaging salt.

ARAUCARIA*	○
Norfolk pine	▲To 70 m
Araucariaceae	

The Norfolk pine, *Araucaria heterophylla*, grows into a large tree, and obviously is unsuited to small gardens, but it is splendid in the right place. Often grown in coastal reserves in Australia and New Zealand, the Norfolk pine is oblivious to coastal gales, and grows equally well in dry sandy soils or clay. It can be started off in a container, and will remain small for some time. Other araucarias can be grown by the sea, but *A. heterophylla* is the best, all parts being covered in a waxy coat. The hoop pine, *A. cunninghamii*, is another most attractive tree for coastal planting.

CORREA	○
Australian fuchsia	▲1 m
Rutaceae	❖ Winter

Correa alba is a hardy member of the family, and rigorous conditions faze it not. Creamy flowers and green leaves, backed grey, are the features of this hardy plant. Not wildly ornamental, just tough and sturdy, *C. alba* can be grown as a hedge. It will not mind salt spray or sandy soil, and is easily propagated from cuttings.

GREVILLEA	○
Proteaceae	▲Prostrate; to 30 m
	❖ Year round

Ranging in size from groundcovers to trees, many grevilleas are splendid for seaside sites. Nearly all are native to Australia, demand well-drained soil and can put up with adverse conditions. Easily hybridised, grevilleas are becoming deservedly popular. Silky oak, *Grevillea robusta*, matures to a large tree, has spectacular flowerheads, and is quick growing. Not suitable for a small garden, the silky oak is one of the biggest grevilleas.

*Dappled shade is used to good
effect in three gardens from
quite dissimilar climates.*

RIGHT: *Daffodils naturalise quickly under deciduous trees in a country garden.*

BELOW: *Trees and shrubs are combined to create a distinctive corner.*

Prostrate forms of grevillea are described in Chapter 1. Varieties include 'Robyn Gordon' with bright red flowers. The brilliant hybrid 'Honey Gem' has bright orange brushes, tipped pink, and is fast-growing and hardy.

GRISELINIA*	◖◗
Broadleaf	▲To 4 m
Cornaceae	❖ Spring

A native of New Zealand, fast-growing *Griselinia littoralis* is tough, with strong, sparkling, bright green leaves. It is often used for shelter hedges as it grows densely. Griselinias produce insignificant flowers, but are handsome shrubs and highly resistant to salt spray and wind. Propagate from cuttings.

LAGUNARIA*	◖◗
Norfolk Island hibiscus	▲To 16 m
Malvaceae	❖ Spring–summer

If a quick-growing large tree is needed in a windy, coastal situation, *Lagunaria patersonii* will fit the bill. This tree has grey, felted leaves, an attractive habit, and lilac, satiny, hibiscus-type flowers. These are profuse and although not startlingly beautiful, are produced for months. Coming from an island with strong winds, *L. patersonii* does not resent them, but it does not like frosty conditions or cold winters.

LEUCADENDRON	◯
Proteaceae	▲1–6 m
	❖ Winter–spring

The spectacular, fast-growing silver tree, *Leucadendron argenteum*, used to be seen in abundance on the hillsides of South Africa's windy Cape Peninsula. If conditions are not too humid, it does extremely well on our coasts too, although it is not long lived. The shimmering silver leaves glint as the wind catches them.

Many other leucadendron species are suitable for coastal planting. Try *L. salignum*, *L. salicifolium* and *L. laureolum*. 'Safari Sunset', a favourite leucadendron, needs more shelter. Leucadendrons like well-drained soil, and not too heavy a rainfall. Propagation is by seed or by cuttings.

METROSIDEROS*	◖◗
New Zealand Christmas tree; pohutukawa	▲To 30 m
Myrtaceae	❖ Summer

The pohutukawa, *Metrosideros excelsa*, is so much at home by the sea that it grows right on the water's edge, almost dipping into it. Happy except in the coldest sea-side places, pohutukawa produces flowers of brightest red, subtly differing from tree to tree. These gold-tipped flowers cover the whole tree. Named varieties are now available — watch out for 'Picta' and 'Variegata'. A yellow-flowered pohutukawa, M. *excelsa* 'Aurea' is also available.

A smaller but equally pleasing tree is the Kermadec Island pohutukawa, M. *kermadacensis*, with lighter leaves and lighter red flowers which are liable to be produced at any time, though generally in summer. Pohutukawa will deal with the strongest winds and it is child's play to grow them. They seed with reckless abandon, and every seed will germinate.

OTHER TREES AND SHRUBS SUITABLE FOR GROWING BY THE SEA
(Those marked with an asterisk* are the first line of defence and shelter from salt winds.)

Acacia — wattle	Lantana camara hybrids
Agonis flexuosa — willow myrtle	Leptospermum — manuka; teatree
Alectryon — titoki	Leucospermum
Arbutus unedo — Irish strawberry tree	Melaleuca
Banksia	Meryta — puka
Buddleia salvifolia — butterfly bush	Myoporum laetum — ngaio*
Callistemon — bottlebrush	Olearia traversii — tree daisy*
Cassia corymbosa	Phoenix canariensis — phoenix palm
Casuarina — sheoke*	Pittosporum crassifolium — karo
Cistus — rock rose	Polygala
Coprosma repens — mirror plant	Psoralea
Cordyline australis — cabbage tree	Rhaphiolepis — Indian hawthorn
Corokia*	Rosmarinus — rosemary
Corynocarpus laevigatus — karaka	Sophora — kowhai
Cupressus arizonica, C. macrocarpa, C. sempervirens	Tamarix*
Entelea — whau	Teucrium fruticans — germander
Feijoa	Virgilia
Hebe	Vitex lucens — puriri
Hibiscus rosa-sinensis and hybrids	Westringia — coast rosemary*

Climbers for seaside gardens

Seaside climbers have a great deal to contend with, for these plants are vulnerable to strong winds and need good support and shelter, especially when young. Salt-laden winds are damaging and inhibit growth, so only strong climbers can survive at sea level. Those marked with an asterisk* are able to withstand fierce, salt-laden winds.

BOUGAINVILLEA ○

Nyctaginaceae ▲3–9 m

❖ Spring–autumn

Bougainvillea look just right growing by the coast, their brilliant bracts contrasting so well with the sea and the sky. *Bougainvillea magnifica* 'Traillii' is the hardiest, but has vicious thorns, grows rampantly and its strident magenta colour does not please everybody. Steadfast red variety 'Scarlet O'Hara' is hardy and lusty. If the wind is too fierce, bougainvillea flag, but they recover remarkably quickly. Both single and double varieties are available in hot and exuberant colours, and new varieties are appearing yearly. In summer bougainvillea like water and the comfort of a mulch.

SOLANDRA* ○

Cup of gold; chalice vine ▲4–10 m

Solanaceae ❖ Spring–summer

This vine, *Solandra guttata*, being strong and lusty, soon gets out of hand, so unless you can provide it with a large area, forget it. The chalice vine is at home by the sea, for it does not like frost and needs warmth. The flowers are very large golden-yellow fleshy cups. Solandra is very easy to propagate from cuttings, and can be grown successfully on large banks, but be warned, it will envelope anything in its path.

TECOMANTHE* ○◐

Bignoniaceae ▲3–5 m

❖ Winter

Tecomanthe hillii is a vigorous climber. The rose-pink trumpet flowers with interior lines of purple are produced in showy clusters, and the leaves are bold, shiny and handsome, deeply green with serrated margins. Tecomanthe flower spasmodically through the year. The vine will not tolerate more than a whisper of frost, is happier in a sheltered position in part shade and can be grown easily from cuttings. *T. speciosa*, a native of New Zealand, with yellow trumpet flowers, is also worth considering.

THUNBERGIA ○

Acanthaceae ▲2–4 m

❖ Year round

Several thunbergias are sturdy enough for life by the sea. Black-eyed Susan, *Thunbergia alata*, will do very well there, as will golden glory creeper, *T. gregorii* (syn. *T. gibsonii*). *T. alata* has flat-faced orange flowers with a distinct black eye. It is available also in yellow and white forms and can be treated as an annual in cold areas. *T. gregorii* is even more brilliant than *T. alata*, and can get out of hand. Both species cohabit with other climbers, and *T. gregorii* makes a good ground-cover. Both are easily propagated from seed.

OTHER CLIMBERS SUITABLE FOR GROWING BY THE SEA
(Those marked with an asterisk* will withstand salt-laden winds.)

Aloe ciliaris — climbing aloe*
Ficus pumila — creeping fig*
Gloriosa — glory lily
Hardenbergia — false sarsaparilla
Hedera — ivy*
Hibbertia scandens — guinea gold vine*
*Jasminum azoricum**

Lathyrus pubescens — Argentine pea
Petrea volubilis — purple wreath
Phaedranthus buccinatorius — Mexican trumpet *
Podranea ricasoliana — pink trumpet climber
Pyrostegia venusta — golden shower

Perennials for seaside gardens

Sturdy perennials are legion, and more than you would imagine are able to put up with salty breezes, including the silver-leaved subjects for a start. Many perennials suitable for growing on banks and in dry gardens (see Chapters 1 and 8) are also good by the sea. After strong salt winds, do not forget to hose down your plants to help the leaves withstand burning, and do mulch seaside perennials.

ARTHROPODIUM	◑●
Renga renga; rock lily	▲75 cm
Liliaceae	❖ Late spring

A New Zealand native which could be useful in street plantings and under trees, *Arthropodium cirrhatum* has graceful sprays of white flowers, does not care for frosts and is at its best in clumps or drifts. Renga renga grows naturally on sea cliffs, so takes salt winds in its stride, and will thrive under trees. It is propagated by division.

CENTRANTHUS	○
Valerian	▲40–90 cm
Valerianaceae	❖ Summer

Valerian, *Centranthus ruber*, is a tough plant for many different places and conditions. Pink, white or red-flowering, this herb naturalises in seaside areas, even in heavy clay soils, and it is almost drought-proof. It is an excellent choice for cracks and crevices, for cottage gardens, any awkward place, and is a treasure in an English meadow garden. It seeds in a lavish way.

ECHIUM	○
Pride of Madiera	▲1–1.5 m
Boraginaceae	❖ Spring–summer

Echium fatuosum, from the Canary Islands, produces impressive spikes of deep lavender-blue flowers. It is very easy to grow in most soils, and although it can become leggy and untidy, it is worth growing for its tolerance of harsh conditions. Bees love it. Propagate from seed.

KNIPHOFIA	○
Hot poker; torch lily	▲To 1.2 m
Liliaceae	❖ Year round

Special hybrids of kniphofia are available in cream, lemon, gold, red and yellow, and will flower at various times of the year, including early winter. All are at home at the beach in sandy or clay soil, but need room as they become large. Birds are attracted to their nectar. Propagate by division.

PHORMIUM	○◐
New Zealand flax	▲To 2.5 m
Agavaceae	❖ Summer

What stalwart plants are New Zealand flaxes! They are survivors, thriving and growing in windy, hostile sites in dry or wet conditions. There are two species, *Phormium tenax* and mountain flax, *P. cookianum*. The hybrids are specially fine, many having weeping leaves and striking colours. Some are in soft pink shades, and two or even three tones, such as the striped yellow leaves margined with red of *P. cookianum* 'Tricolor'. New Zealand flax is easily propagated by division, and is a most versatile and handsome plant. The large prominent flowerheads are filled with nectar and thus much visited by birds.

OTHER PERENNIALS SUITABLE FOR SEASIDE GARDENS

Agapanthus
Aloe
Arctotis — African daisy
Artemisia
Astelia
Cortaderia — pampas grass
Eryngium — sea holly
Felicia amelloides — blue marguerite
Gazania
Hemerocallis — day lily
Lampranthus — ice plant
Myosotidium — Chatham Island forget-me-not
Osteospermum
Scaevola — fan flower
Sedum — stonecrop
Sempervivium — houseleek
Viola hederaceae — Australian native violet
Xeronema — Poor Knights lily

Bulbs for seaside gardens

Dry, sandy soil and salt winds do not seem suitable for bulb growing. However, some of the tough South Africans grow naturally right by the sea. In fact, some bulbs have naturalised on the coast in many Southern Hemisphere countries. Those described in Chapter 8 for dry gardens are also good by the sea.

FREESIA	◯◑
Iridaceae	▲To 35 cm
	❖ Spring

Freesia corms multiply smartly, and if given a touch of blood and bone at planting time, these will do admirably by the sea. Salt winds do not affect them much, although the large hybrids flop and need support. *Freesia burtonii* is still deservedly popular, and *F. refracta* is the familiar, hardy, fragrant freesia with cream flowers which naturalises in many places right to the sea edge.

SPARAXIS	◯◑
Iridaceae	▲30 cm
	❖ Spring

Sparaxis are brilliantly coloured in clear orange, red, pink, purple and cream. The flowers grow on top of a wiry stem and the leaves are very like those of freesias. Very hardy, sparaxis are best grown in large clumps near shrubs to shelter them from the harshest winds. *Sparaxis tricolor* is the finest species. Propagate from seed.

OTHER BULBS SUITABLE FOR GROWING BY THE SEA

Allium — ornamental onion
Amaryllis — belladonna lily
Babiana — baboon flower
Crinum

Ixia
Tritonia
Watsonia — bugle lily

Annuals for seaside gardens

Annuals to grow by the sea include many which survive on banks and other dry alien areas (see Chapters 1 and 8). The hardiest will withstand strong sea winds and tolerate poor soils.

HIBISCUS	◯
Malvaceae	▲35 cm
	❖ Summer–autumn

Often an annual, sometimes a biennial, *Hibiscus trionum* is native to both Australia and New Zealand. The creamy flowers with a deep wine centre are unusual in colour and most effective in the cottage or beach garden. This hibiscus seeds freely, forming handsome seedheads. Best planted in groups, *H. trionum* looks well grown under shrubs in coastal situations.

LIMONIUM	○
Statice	▲45 cm
Plumbaginaceae	❖ Spring–summer

Good for dried arrangements, *Limonium sinuatum* are available in a lovely blend of colours from white to purple, and in apricot and yellow. It is the bracts surrounding the insignificant flowers which are so colourful. Statice is not fussy over soil, as long as it is well-drained, but the plants need to be staked in exposed situations. And watch out for rust — they are martyrs to it.

MESEMBRYANTHEMUM	○
Livingstone daisy	▲15 cm
Aizoaceae	❖ Spring

Light soil suits Livingstone daisies. Their dazzling flowers need full sun, as even on a cloudy day they refuse to open. They like warmth and do very well in containers. As they hug the ground, winds do not worry them too much. Easily propagated from seed, Livingstone daisies are good on banks and in rock gardens.

OTHER ANNUALS SUITABLE FOR GROWING BY THE SEA

Dimorpotheca — star of the veldt
Eschscholzia — California poppy
Glaucium — horned poppy
Lagurus — hare's tail

Lobularia — sweet alyssum
Petunia
Senecio maritima — dusty miller
Tropaeolum — nasturtium

Hibiscus

WATER GARDENS

10

Water in the garden has captivated people since early times. The Egyptians designed pools for growing water lilies and the sacred lotus. Water is a most desirable asset in any garden from the design viewpoint, and is also most beneficial to all plants growing there, for it creates extra humidity.

Water gardens are a planned environment for plants which thrive in wet, marshy areas, on stream banks or in pools. Although the aspect will govern the planting, it is not difficult to create a lush, sultry atmosphere with waterside plants and aquatics for the pool.

Soils generally are not very fertile in damp or wet areas so if you are considering transforming such a site into a garden, be prepared to add compost and well-rotted animal manures, and feed your more special plants regularly, e.g. primulas and iris.

BOG GARDENS AND POOL MARGINS

Anyone with still water and damp places in the garden is indeed fortunate. Many plants with lush, exotic, bold foliage revel in such conditions, as well as certain others with fine flowers. A wet, marshy area can support a rich variety of plant life, and despite its unpromising name, the bog garden is often the most appealing part of a property.

Bog gardens and pool margins need to be generously planted in clumps and drifts. Other than stepping stones for ease of access or maybe a boardwalk and simple plank or oriental bridge, plants are usually the only embellishment necessary.

Trees and shrubs for damp or wet areas

If the marshy area is large enough, there will be room in your bog garden for trees and shrubs. Although not many are adapted to a damp life, those that are do extremely well.

ACACIA	◯◗
Wattle	▲2 m
Leguminosae	❖ Spring

Acacia riceana has yellow flowers and a neat, bushy habit. It appreciates cool conditions and relishes moisture. Acacias are a versatile genus and many like the exact opposite of these conditions.

CASUARINA	◯◗
Sheoke; swamp oak	▲4–20 m
Casuarinaceae	

The adaptable sheokes put up with harsh conditions. Swamp oak, *Casuarina glauca*, will grow in bogs, and has deep-green handsome foliage.

PERNETTYA	◯◗
Ericaceae	▲1 m
	❖ Spring–summer

A wiry, evergreen shrub from Chile, *Pernettya mucronata* will thrive in damp, peaty soil. It has heath-like pretty white flowers and handsome berries. *P. mucronata* can be transplanted at any stage, and is propagated easily by cuttings.

SALIX	◯
Willow	▲4 m
Salicaceae	

Weeping willow, *Salix babylonica*, is ideal for pool margins and damp conditions in a large garden. This deciduous tree is glorious in early spring when its weeping branches are clothed in bright lime-green leaves. It loses its leaves late, and is one of the first trees to burst forth in spring.

TAXODIUM	◯◑
Swamp cypress	▲To 11 m
Taxodiaceae	

Taxodium distichum is deciduous, producing splendid autumn colour. It is a large, majestic tree which will endure frost, but not dry conditions.

OTHER TREES AND SHRUBS SUITABLE FOR BOG GARDENS
Alnus — alder
Cordyline australis — cabbage tree
Cyathea — tree fern
Podocarpus dacrydioides — kahikatea
Quercus palustris — pin oak

Perennials for damp or wet areas

Numerous perennials relish the wet conditions of bog gardens and pool margins.

ARUNCUS	◯
Goat's beard	▲2 m
Rosaceae	❖Late summer

Bold trusses of creamy-white flowers on tall stems distinguish the goat's beard, *Aruncus dioicus*, which is hardy in cool climates. Deeply cut, ornamental leaves, flowers smelling of hay, and seedheads suitable for drying all make this a brilliant subject for bog gardens and pool margins.

ASTILBE	◯◑
Saxifragaceae	▲15 cm–1.2 m
	❖Spring

Long-lived astilbe have plumes of flowers from white, pink, and red through to deep red, and pretty, ferny foliage. Astilbe perform to perfection in moist soil and a shady position. Try any of the many cultivars. Some varieties produce arching sprays of flowers but most are upright. Plant astilbe in drifts with other water-loving perennials. The dried seedheads are eye-catching and useful for dried-flower arrangements.

CALTHA ○

| Marsh marigold | ▲30–45 cm |
| Ranunculaceae | ❖Spring |

Caltha palustris is the marsh marigold. It has shiny, double, buttercup-yellow flowers, and showy, glossy leaves. Marsh marigolds look splendid growing with blue *Iris sibirica* at pool margins.

CIMIFUGA ○●

| Bugbane | ▲1.5 m |
| Ranunculaceae | ❖Summer |

With impressive spikes of greeny-white, feathery flowers on a robust plant, *Cimifuga racemosa* is happily at home in the bog garden. *C. cordifolia* has fragrant flowers, shiny, dark leaves, and is happy basking in the sun. You can grow all cimifugas from seed.

CYPERUS ○◐●

| Papyrus | ▲1–3 m |
| Cyperaceae | |

Papyrus is featured on ancient Egyptian columns and tomb walls. It is a tall-standing foliage plant which revels in moist conditions. Papyrus gives pool margins and damp garden areas an exotic air, and can be planted amidst hostas and arum lilies or a host of other perennials which like wet feet.

FILIPENDULA ○◐

| Meadowsweet | ▲60 cm–1.2 m |
| Rosaceae | ❖Summer |

Meadowsweet, *Filipendula ulmaria*, produces frothy, creamy-white plumes of flowers, and is a most valuable plant for the bog garden. *F. rubra* is another. It bears fine, rosy flowers on tall stems, for all the world like candy-floss, and the leaves are handsome too.

GUNNERA ○◐

| Haloraginaceae | ▲3–3.5 m |
| | ❖Summer |

Gunnera manicata is an impressive, large plant with giant rhubarb-like leaves and conical flowers. It needs a large pool to do it justice and is a good foil for other plants. *G. propens* is of groundcover proportions. It is covered in bright red fruits in autumn.

IRIS	◯◗
Iridaceae	▲60–90 cm
	❖ Spring–summer

One of the many virtues of the bog-garden irises is their agreeable habit of flowering at different times. The hybrid forms of the Louisiana iris, from swampy areas of Louisiana and Florida, are easy to grow, and are one of the first irises to flower in early spring. The new cultivars have large flowers in soft colours of yellow, mauve, pink, and purple. They appreciate compost and manure.

The Japanese iris, *Iris kaempferi*, is spectacular, with glorious flowers like brilliant tropical butterflies. The new cultivars have elegant blooms in rainbow shades. The 'Higo' strain is hard to beat. Japanese iris prefer an acid soil and a position at the pool margin where their roots can reach water.

The Siberian iris, *I. sibirica*, is undemanding but needs fertilising annually and plenty of sun. Siberica hybrids abound in many striking colours — from white through many shades of blue to lemon, lavender and pale pink. *I. laevigata* is the intense blue iris of the paddy fields, and will grow in shallow water. It has innumerable hybrids, including the delicate white 'Alba' and some in two-tone shades. Propagate these iris by division.

LYSICHITON	◯◗
Skunk cabbage	▲1.2 m
Araceae	❖ Spring

With yellow, arum-like flowers, the skunk cabbage, *Lysichiton americanus*, grows equally well in shallow water and at the edge of a pool. It is greedy and likes a lot of room. The leaves are about 1.2 m high, quite massive. Unfortunately the flowers have an unpleasant smell.

PRIMULA	◗
Candelabra primula; drumstick primula	▲30–90 cm
Primulaceae	❖ Spring–late summer

Many members of this bonny family thrive in damp places and beside pool margins. Primulas, along with iris, are the stars of the bog garden, flowering for many months. They come in all shapes and sizes, and many colours. They all dote on rich soil, and are splendid planted in generous drifts. The drumstick primulas include one of the first to flower, *Primula denticulata*, with round, white, pink, mauve or purple flowerheads. Only suitable for cooler climates, the candelabra primulas *P. japonica* and *P. helodoxa* carry their blooms in tiers and whorls on tall spikes. And do not overlook the Sikkimensis primulas with their nodding flowers. Propagate by division and seed.

Primula

SAGITTARIA	○
Arrowhead	▲60–90 cm
Alismataceae	❖ Spring–summer

Good for pool margins, *Sagittaria japonica* is a worthwhile plant. *S. sagittifolia* is another good one, but all sagittarias can become invasive, so beware. In Western Australia several species are prohibited.

ZANTEDESCHIA	○◑
Arum lily	▲90 cm
Araceae	❖ Winter–spring

A good steadfast plant for the bog garden, arums, *Zantedeschia aethiopica*, never fail to please with their white, fleshy spathe and yellow spadix. They combine charmingly with the cool hostas, and also look well in drifts. 'Green Goddess' is splashed with light green. Arums are really only suitable for a large area.

POOLS AND PONDS

Pools and ponds add an extra dimension to the garden, often providing a focal point in its design, and are a source of beauty and interest at any time of year. A pool is a cool oasis, supporting animal and plant life. The sound and sight of water refresh flagging spirits. Tranquil pools are places for contemplation; waterfalls and fountains bring life to the garden in a unique way.

Whatever the style of water garden you plan, when siting a pool do remember that fish and the best aquatic plants need full sun to thrive.

Aquatic plants

Planting a pool is bringing it to life. There must be a balance between water, plants and fish. A rough guide is one waterlily to two fish and an oxygenating plant to each square metre of pool. Underplant — resist the temptation to overdress the pond or pool. To see the reflections of clouds and the movement of fish in the water is reason enough to include a pool in any garden.

One warning — water hyacinth, *Eichhornia crassipes*, is a noxious weed. The urge to grow it is great as it is so pretty. Do not. Nor *Salvinia molesta*, which can choke rivers and lakes. Do not grow either of these two villains. Also keep an eye on oxygenating weeds as they can get away from streams and choke waterways and lakes. And even waterlilies can prove a nuisance.

APONOGETON	○
Cape pondweed; water hawthorn	▲10 cm (above water)
Aponogetonaceae	❖ Spring–autumn

Aponogeton distachyus, from South Africa, has fragrant white flowers which float prettily on the water. They need a 15–25 cm depth of water to grow successfully. Plant as for waterlilies.

HYDROCLEYS ○

Water poppy	▲90 cm
Butomaceae	❖ Summer

The pretty poppy *Hydrocleys nymphoides* produces simple yellow flowers and large, rounded, deep-green leaves. It only needs 15–20 cm of water, and does not tolerate frost. *H. nymphoides* is an aquatic for warm areas.

IRIS ○

Flag iris; water iris	▲1–1.5 m
Iridaceae	❖ Spring

Iris pseudacorus is a true aquatic, and has yellow flowers with stiff leaves. It has a most handsome variety with gold-striped leaves and branched, shiny stems. *I. laevigata* grows in shallow water.

NELUMBO ○

Lotus	▲90 cm–1.8 m
Nymphaeaceae	❖ Summer

The sacred lotus, *Nelumbo nucifera*, is a tropical aquatic and can only be grown in very warm areas and requires a large pool or tub. A spectacular plant with huge fragrant pink flowers followed by large seedheads prized for dried-flower arrangements, the sacred lotus is the prima donna of the warm pool. The leaves are waxy, shaped rather like immense nasturtium leaves. Several varieties are equally beautiful, and the white magnolia lotus is worth searching for. Sacred lotus needs at least 25 cm of water over each plant and a square metre of pool. The pygmy hybrids are quite happy in a small pool or tub, perhaps even a bucket. The American lotus, *N. petapetala* (syn. *N. luteus*), is hardier and has creamy-lemon flowers which hover becomingly above the water.

NYMPHAEA ○

Waterlily	▲To 20 cm (floating)
Nymphaeaceae	❖ Summer–autumn

Revered since ancient times, waterlilies are the stars of the garden pool. They are easy to grow as long as you have 20–60 cm depth of water and room for them to spread. (A rough guide would be one medium-sized waterlily to a square metre of pool.) Waterlilies need full sun. The rhizomes are usually planted in loam-filled, weighted containers with holes in the bottom. The mix can include well-rotted animal manure, and gravel or stones should be placed on top to stop the soil escaping from the container when it is submerged. When you buy waterlilies, growing instructions should be supplied.

The colours of the hardy waterlily varieties include white, pink, red and yellow.

*Clever combinations of line
and structure, and the careful
choice of plants, are tributes to
the designers' skill in these fine
gardens. Cropped hedges and
topiary form interesting
contrasts.*

Good gardeners make use of bountiful planting in their designs. Plants in profusion not only create a generous effect, they also keep down the weeds.

The small pygmy types, suited for growing in smaller pools, come in shades of yellow, hot pink and orange. If you have no other plant in the pool, make sure you have a waterlily.

Blue lotus of the Nile, *Nymphaea caerulea*, a tropical waterlily, has heavenly blue flowers held high above the water. It is one of the easiest tropical waterlilies to cultivate and can be grown in a tub on a warm terrace. It needs 45–75 cm depth of water. Other day-blooming tropical waterlilies are available and the colour range is larger than provided by their hardier cousins — a kaleidoscope of colours no less, with many glorious blues.

OXYGENATORS

Care must be taken with oxygen plants in the pool to ensure they are contained. The oxygen weed, *Elodia canadensis*, is an efficient oxygenator. Oxygenators and aquatics with floating flowers and anchored, flowering plants and fish create a balanced environment. Oxygenating plants enliven the water by emission of oxygen through leaf pores, using up carbon dioxide and taking food from lowly, unwelcome algae. Do not grow *Lagarosiphon major*.

PONTEDERIA	○
Pickerel weed	▲60–90 cm
Pontederiaceae	❖ Summer

Pontederia cordata has upright blue flowers and handsome, philodendron-like leaves. *P. cordata* grows rather rampantly but is easily restricted, and is best for a large, shallow pool.

OTHER AQUATICS SUITABLE FOR THE POOL AND POND
Hydrocharis — frogbit   *Orontium aquaticum* — golden
Nuphar lutea — brandy bottle   club
Nymphoides peltata — water fringe   Thalia — water canna

IN THE SHADE

11

At first glance a liability, a shady garden can in fact become a home for many beautiful plants. Such a place is often more interesting than the sunny garden, for shade provides a cool oasis and growing conditions suited to some very fascinating species. Some shady areas are dry due to overhanging house eaves, or heavy trees; others are cool and damp. Dramatic foliage plants, ferns and a wide range of flowering subjects are suited to the damp shade garden. For more arid areas, fewer plants are ideal, but some are designed to survive shade and dry conditions.

Most importantly, shade gardens supply intriguing planes and shadows, secret gardens, arbours and bowers, quiet spots for hammocks and seats, retreats from the world. From earliest times humans have desired shade and shelter away from the dwelling, a private place to cool off and contemplate the world outside. A shady garden fills this need admirably.

Trees and shrubs to grow in shaded areas

Many trees and shrubs are happy in shade, but keep them small and decorative. Large trees will create more shade and will take much-needed nutrients out of the soil. Valuable light in winter will be increased if you use a few deciduous varieties in your planting.

AZALEA	◖●
Ericaceae	▲To 1.8 m
	❖ Spring

Drifts of brilliantly coloured azaleas under large trees make a memorable sight. Azaleas are rhododendrons really, but it is confusing to lump them all together. Indica azaleas, evergreens, flower in colours of white, pink, mauve and red, both single and double. Kurume azaleas are free-flowering, more compact, and will endure colder conditions. Azaleas need acid, deep rich soil and appreciate water on their foliage as well as roots in hot periods. Azalea flowers smother the bush and stay in flower for a month or more. Adaptable, they grow very well in pots on the shady deck or patio. The deciduous azaleas like to be in more sun, and are for cool areas only.

Azalea

CYATHEA ◖●

Tree fern ▲3–15 m

Cyatheaceae

The rough tree fern, *Cyathea australis,* is probably the most suitable species of tree fern for garden growing. The handsome ponga fern *C. dealbata,* is also perfectly happy in a domestic situation provided it has moist soil and half shade. Shelter is most important; strong winds are anathema to tree ferns. The black tree fern, *C. medullaris,* occurs in the Pacific, parts of Australia and New Zealand, and is quick growing. *C. medullaris* likes the same conditions as the ponga fern, but needs more room. All tree ferns need water when conditions are dry — water their trunks, they will appreciate it. Any number of perennials, bromeliads and groundcovers can be grown under tree ferns. They do not take much goodness from the soil — in fact, they appear to benefit their surroundings.

DACRYDIUM ◖●

Rimu ▲10 m

Podocarpaceae

Rimu, *Dacrydium cupressinum,* is one of New Zealand's prettiest native trees. It can be used as a specimen, but is perfect in the shady bush. It is slow growing, and although it ultimately attains a great height, in the home garden it will be in bounds for many years. The foliage is ethereal and cypress-like, hanging in long sprays. Rimu appreciates moist conditions. Ferns, hostas, and hellebores look very well growing under rimu.

FATSIA ◖●

Aralia ▲1–2 m

Araliaceae ❖ Spring

The ubiquitous *Fatsia japonica* tends to be forgotten today, yet it gives no trouble and is a good shrub for the shade garden. It appears to have no enemies, and grows quickly. The flowers are unusual, a rounded, greeny-white, but it is the foliage the fatsia is grown for. Its deep-green, shiny, divided leaves always look well, and never become bedraggled. Grow a fatsia under a tree, and try *Fatshedera lizei,* a hybrid of *F. japonica* and *Hedera helix,* for a really eye-catching specimen.

HYDRANGEA ◐◖

Saxifragaceae ▲1–2 m

❖ Spring–summer

Hydrangea macrophylla and its cultivars are the deciduous bushy type, so popular and deservedly so. Hydrangeas can be used as a hedge or just planted to be admired in the shade garden. Superbly showy, the flowers are white, pink, mauve, and all shades of blue. They fade to greens, bronzes, richest wines and deep slate blue. If you want blue hydrangeas, plant them in acid soil. To encourage pink colours, give them an annual dressing of lime. Prune in winter, and plant the healthy cuttings — it is simplicity itself to get them to grow. *H. quercifolia* has white flowers and in autumn the oak-shaped leaves brighten. *H. paniculata* 'Grandiflora' is very hardy and very beautiful, with large heads of white flowers which fade to pink (see Chapter 2). Hydrangeas also make excellent tub specimens for less sunny corners of the terrace, or for using as focal points in the shade garden.

KALMIA	◑
Calico bush	▲3 m
Ericaceae	❖ Spring

What a charming sight this shrub is when in flower. For all the world like pink icing piped on to the bush, kalmia buds open to starry flowers. Only good in cool areas, *Kalmia latifolia* grows wild in many states of the US — North Carolina for one. Kalmias like company — two or three grown near azaleas and rhododendrons, all acid lovers, would be ideal.

RHODODENDRON	◑
Ericaceae	▲1–9 m
	❖ Spring–summer

Another member of the esteemed Ericaceae family, rhododendrons have a large following and are amongst the most brilliant of the spring-flowering shrubs. Perhaps it is prodigal to grow rhododendrons in a small garden, as once they have done their dash, they are rather gloomy shrubs. However, when they are in flower they are so beautiful, few can resist their charms.

OTHER TREES AND SHRUBS SUITABLE FOR SHADY GARDENS
(Those marked with an asterisk* grow in deep shade.)

Abutilon — Chinese lantern
Acer — maple
Aucuba*
Azara
Boronia
Camellia
Choisya — Mexican orange blossom
Cornus florida — flowering
    dogwood
Cycas*
Daphne
Dicksonia — tree fern*
Enkianthus

Epacris — Australian native fuchsia
Eriostemon — waxflower
Fuchsia
Halesia — snowdrop tree
Kerria
Pernettya
Philadelphus — mock orange
Pieris — lily-of-the-valley shrub
Rhopalostylis — nikau palm*
Ruscus — butcher's broom*
Sarcococca — sweet box*
Schefflera digitata — pate
Viburnum

Climbers for shaded areas

Many climbers in nature grow under trees and shrubs with their roots in the cool shade. Often they strive to climb up the trees to get to the light and warmth, but some climbers need little or no sun at all.

CELASTRUS	◑●
Climbing bittersweet	▲6 m
Celastraceae	❖ Summer

Celastrus scandens is ultra-hardy. It is a rampant deciduous climber, often seen scrambling up trees, and is grown for its golden berries. These open in autumn to reveal pillar-box red seeds. Not only that, the leaves turn butter-yellow in cold climates before they fall. *C. scandens* does not need a partner to produce berries. Pick the sprays of berries for winter decoration.

CLEMATIS	◑
Ranunculaceae	▲To 10 m
	❖ Spring–autumn

Only hardy clematis are mentioned here, but this brilliant genus has over 250 species, and many are content in the shade. Evergreen *Clematis armandii* has flowers of pure white contrasting well with the deep green, glossy leaves. *Clematis montana* is a vigorous plant bearing masses of white, single, four-petalled flowers. *C. montana* 'Rubens' is a rosy-pink cultivar. *C. flammula* is an enchanting white deciduous clematis, summer flowering and so pretty. All these climbers have appeal, but the large-flowered hybrids in glorious colours need a lot of care.

HYDRANGEA	◑●
Climbing hydrangea	▲6 m
Saxifragaceae	❖ Summer

The best known of the climbing types of the genus is *Hydrangea petiolaris*, a lacecap type of deciduous hydrangea with creamy flowers. It grows up trees with ease, attaching itself by aerial rootlets. *H. serratifolia* (syn. *H. integerrima*) is evergreen, with domed panicles of rich cream flowers and dark green leaves. Climbing hydrangeas grow best in situations similar to those enjoyed by ordinary garden hydrangeas, and are just as easy to propagate from cuttings.

LAPAGERIA	●
Chilean bellflower	▲2–3 m
Liliaceae	❖ Summer–autumn

This is the national flower of Chile, and no wonder, for lapageria blooms are perfect.

Lapageria rosea grows with rapidity, producing rosy-red, heavy trumpets which go on blooming for a long while. 'Albiflora' is white flowered of course. These bell-flowers demand shade, a rich, acid soil and a climate with a generous rainfall. A south-facing wall suits them, and a yearly mulch is beneficial.

SCHIZOPHRAGMA	◑●
Saxifragaceae	▲6 m
	❖ Summer

Slow growing to begin with, and a relation of the hydrangea, *Schizophragma hydrangeoides* is a handsome climber with large cream flowerheads. One variety has bracts slightly pink. Propagate by layering.

OTHER CLIMBERS SUITABLE FOR SHADY AREAS
(Those marked with an asterisk* grow in deep shade.)

Billardiera longiflora — purple apple berry
Ficus pumila — creeping fig*
Hardenbergia — false sarsaparilla

Hedera — ivy*
Monstera — fruit-salad plant
Metrosideros carminea — climbing rata
Stephanotis — Madagascar jasmine

Perennials for shaded gardens

Dozens of the best perennials can be grown in the shade garden, although many of the large-leaved types demand moist conditions. Ferns with their filigree foliage complement hostas, hellebores, and the like. Perennials establish quickly and well, and often last many years in the shady garden. They are invaluable for growing under trees and shrubs.

ALCHEMILLA	○◐
Lady's mantle	▲25 cm
Rosaceae	❖ Spring

Easy to grow, and adaptable, *Alchemilla mollis* has pretty glaucous foliage on which raindrops settle as if drops of quicksilver. The yellow-green dainty sprays of flowers froth over the plant, last obligingly and are excellent when dried for flower arrangements. *A. mollis* can be used as a groundcover between shrubs, but does not like it too dry. It seeds recklessly and can be planted in sun in cool climates. Lady's mantle complements other flowers, especially those with white, blue and yellow blooms.

AQUILEGIA	◐
Columbine	▲To 75 cm
Ranunculaceae	❖ Spring

Winsome, old-fashioned columbines, aquilegias with quaint flowerheads in unusual colours, feature long spurs and graceful flowers. The Victorian columbines are back in fashion, but the hybrids have bigger blooms and come in some amazing colour combinations. Aquilegias are easily raised from seed, and appreciate filtered shade. The species self-seed most satisfactorily.

BILBERGIA	◐
Bromeliaceae	▲50 cm
	❖ Spring

Bromeliads are a fascinating lot, with bizarre flowers and colours. Most of them enjoy shady conditions and relish humidity. Not for the dry garden, all bilbergias are as unusual as other members of the family, with flowers in combinations of pink, blue, green and yellow. Try other bromeliads too. They will grow on tree ferns, under trees and in containers. Buy bromeliads from specialist nurseries.

HELLEBORUS	◐●
Ranunculaceae	▲To 1 m
	❖ Winter–spring

Can there be anybody who dislikes hellebores? It would be difficult to imagine. *Helleborus lividus corsicus* has cups of delicate green, similar to the finest translucent porcelain. *H. foetidus* is another for gardeners partial to green flowers. And then there's spotted *H. orientalis* and its many hybrids, which have flowers of red, pink, maroon and white. Hellebores ask for little. Grown under trees in well-drained soil with plenty of leafmould, they will thrive. All have attractive foliage, and some are deciduous. You can propagate them by division. Hellebores are a promiscuous lot, integrating well and sometimes producing surprising offspring.

HOSTA	◐●
Plantain lily	▲To 90 cm
Liliaceae	❖ Summer

Hostas will grow in fertile, damp areas and are very much at home on the margins of pools or in the bog garden as well as in shady spots. They are grown for their impressive foliage, although they do produce spikes of light lilac flowers. *Hosta fortunei* is one of the largest and has thick, grey-green bold leaves. Some hostas are splashed with cream, others, such as *H. sieboldiana*, have clear cream or gold edges. Martyrs to slugs and snails, hostas must be protected when they emerge from the ground. They die down in winter.

MYOSOTIDIUM	◐●
Chatham Island forget-me-not	▲To 60 cm
Boraginaceae	❖Spring

Even without flowers, the Chatham Island forget-me-not, *Myosotidium hortensia*, would be worth growing, for its leaves are deeply veined, shiny and bold. The flowers are a breathtaking, heavenly blue with a dark cobalt-blue eye, rivalling any blue flower in cultivation. Give *M. hortensia* filtered shade and well-drained soil. Some say give them lime, others not. Seaweed and well-rotted fish boosts them along, as their natural habitat is right on the coast. Grow from fresh seed sown in February; they should flower in 18 months with green fingers and luck.

THALICTRUM	○◗
Meadow rue	▲To 1.5 m
Ranunculaceae	❖Summer

Pretty *Thalictrum aquilegifolium* is a stalwart plant for the shade garden. It is a good mixer and grows well amongst others. The fluffy flowerheads are rosy mauve or white. *T. dipterocarpum* has lavender flowerheads and ferny foliage. All thalictrums like well-drained soil, and all are easily raised from seed or division. There are several yellow-flowered species. All are good for cutting and can be propagated from seed.

OTHER PERENNIALS SUITABLE FOR SHADED GARDENS
(Those marked with an asterisk* will grow in deep shade.)

Aconitum — aconite; monkshood
Agapanthus*
Ajuga — bugle
Alocasia — elephant's ear*
Anemone — Japanese; wood
    anenome; *A. blanda*
Aruncus — goat's beard
Astilbe
Begonia
Bergenia
Cimifuga — bugbane
Dicentra — bleeding heart
Hemerocallis — day lily
Incarvillea

Liriope — lily turf*
Mazus
Meconopsis betonicifolia —
    Himalayan blue poppy
Mertensia
Parochetus — shamrock pea*
Phyllostachys nigra — black
    bamboo*
Polygonatum — Solomon's seal
Primula
Tiarella — foam flower
Tricyrtis — toad lily
Viola — violet

Bulbs for shaded gardens

Many bulbs thrive in the shade, and in dappled shade woodland bulbs excel. As they grow they need good drainage and only a modest amount of fertiliser. In the shady garden bulbs look more natural when planted in companionable drifts and clumps of one species.

CARDIOCRINUM

Liliaceae ▲3 m

❖ Early–mid summer

True to name, *Cardiocrinum giganteum* is an enormous plant bearing trumpets of creamy-white flowers on huge, sturdy stems. It takes several years to reach flowering point. The leaves are immense ovals. A majestic sight, not to be forgotten when in flower, cardiocrinums look best amongst trees and shrubs in a cool, humus-rich, moist soil, though well-drained. They do have a few drawbacks, a major one being that the bulbs die after flowering. They do leave offsets, but you should plant bulbs of different sizes each year to ensure flowers.

CLIVIA

Kaffir lily ▲85 cm

Amaryllidaceae ❖ Spring

Bearing handsome apricot flowers on sturdy stems, surrounded by deep green, strap-like leaves, *Clivia miniata* is a paragon for shade gardens. In very cold climates clivias are eminently suited to tub-growing on a shady terrace. *C. miniata* is at home under trees. Clivias like a comforting mulch, are slightly affected by frost, and take a while to get established. Once you have them, you have them for life.

CYCLAMEN

Primulaceae ▲10 cm

❖ Autumn–spring

Delightful *Cyclamen hederifolium* (syn. *C. neapolitinum*) with small, fly-away flowers, can be naturalised in a shady, well-drained soil under trees. Cyclamen do not like being disturbed. Flowers are pink or white, and shoot up before the heart-shaped, marbled leaves. *C. coum* blooms later and has fat flowers from pale to deep pink. A bonus, *C. coum* seeds wonderfully well. A new silver-leaved form has appeared.

ERYTHRONIUM

Dog's-tooth violet ▲15–20 cm

Liliaceae ❖ Spring

If you can grow these woodland plants, you are indeed fortunate. They like cold winters. However, in warm areas, if given cold, shady conditions, they can do well. As do many woodland species, *Erythronium dens-canis* enjoys humus and moist, well-drained soil, and is unhappy in hot summers. Erythroniums like company and are best planted in clumps.

LEUCOJUM	◐◑
Snowflake	▲ 30 cm
Amaryllidaceae	❖ Winter–summer

Snowflakes are so hardy they naturalise and are to be seen in fields and paddocks, sometimes the only reminder that once a house stood there. Pretty, nodding white flowers with green, jewel-like tips *Leucojum vernum* is happy under trees and amongst grass. *L. vernum* flowers early, *L. aestivum* is later, and *L. autumnale*, a sweet wee thing, is a summer version.

OTHER BULBS SUITABLE FOR SHADED AREAS
(Those marked with an asterisk* will grow in deep shade.)

Arisaema*	Galanthus — snowdrop
Arisarum — mouse plant*	Muscari — grape hyacinth
Endymion (syn. Scilla) — bluebell	Narcissus
Fritillaria	Scilla

Annuals for shady gardens

Hardy annuals germinate at low temperatures and are best sown in autumn to flower in spring and summer. In the shade garden annuals add colour and warmth, and a surprising number do well in such situations, provided they have well-drained soil.

DIGITALIS	◐◑●
Foxglove	▲ 1 m
Scrophulariaceae	❖ Spring–summer

Hardy perennials (or biennials) and annuals, foxgloves, *Digitalis purpurea*, are very easy to grow, and the flower colours are delightful, ranging from white, pink, mauve and purple to cream and lemon, with winsome spots. Annual 'Foxy' will flower 5 months from sowing. All foxgloves will self-seed in damp soils. They are at their best amidst taller shrubs or other cottage-garden plants, and with old-fashioned roses.

IMPATIENS	◑●
Busy Lizzie	▲ To 75 cm
Balsaminaceae	❖ Year round

The modern impatiens are mainly the result of hybridising. The colours are glowing and brilliant, and their importance in the home garden cannot be overemphasised. Usually they are treated as annuals, but in the warm garden impatiens will last for years. The rose-like double varieties need more tender care and are best grown in pots on a shady terrace (see Chapter 6). Impatiens will flower all year long where humidity, warmth and shade can be provided. New hybrids are appearing yearly as growers realise the immense potential of this plant. The colour range is large and pleasing, the pure white for some reason being the most delicate to grow. Impatiens act as barometer plants, being the first to wilt when the soil is too dry.

LUNARIA	◐●
Honesty	▲75 cm
Cruciferae	❖ Spring–summer

Honesty, *Lunaria annua*, is prized mainly for its mother-of-pearl oval seedpods, which appear in summer and autumn. The flowers are available in white (a most effective colour for the shade garden), pink and mauve. Honesty seeds with no trouble.

MYOSOTIS	◐●
Forget-me-not	▲To 15 cm
Boraginaceae	❖ Spring

Forget-me-nots, *Myosotis sylvatica*, will naturalise in your shade garden, given half a chance. The usual colour is sky blue, but try to obtain the white, pink and deep-blue varieties as well. The seed germinates with remarkable ease, and forget-me-nots transplant well. Moist soil suits them, and they are not fussy as to types, growing well in clay.

SENECIO	◐●
Cineraria	▲To 1 m
Compositae	❖ Winter–spring

Cinerarias, *Senecio cruentus*, are perhaps the best-loved annuals for the shade garden. In royal colours of rich purple, blue and velvety-red, cinerarias romp away under shrubs and trees, or when intermingled with more sober plants. Frost tender, cinerarias in cool climates should be set out to flower late in the season. Sow the seed in autumn. Cinerarias self-sow and naturalise in warm areas. They thrive if well fed.

OTHER ANNUALS SUITABLE FOR SHADED GARDENS
(Those marked with an asterisk* will grow in deep shade.)

Adonis — pheasant's eye
Campanula — Canterbury bells
Coleus*
Limnanthes douglasii — meadow
    foam

Lobelia
Mimulus — monkey flower
Nemophila — baby-blue-eyes
Nigella — love-in-a-mist
Primula malacoides — fairy
    primula

WILDFLOWER
AND
BUSH GARDENS

12

WILDFLOWER MEADOW GARDENS • Perennials for naturalising • Bulbs for naturalising • Annuals for naturalising • A BUSH GARDEN OF AUSTRALIAN PLANTS • Australian trees and shrubs • Australian climbers • Australian perennials • Australian annuals • A BUSH GARDEN OF NEW ZEALAND PLANTS • New Zealand trees and shrubs • New Zealand climbers • New Zealand perennials

---

There is world-wide concern at the loss of indigenous plants in the wild, and gardeners are becoming increasingly interested in gardens inspired by the flora of their own country; gardens to protect the environment — wildflower and native-bush gardens. Wildflowers attract bees and butterflies whilst bush gardens temper the atmosphere, help deal with pollution and are havens for birds.

Such low-maintenance, wild, natural retreats often offer gardeners solutions for problem areas. You can choose introduced species when creating a wildflower meadow, but the bush garden will most likely feature either Australian or New Zealand plants, or a mixture of both. These plants are constantly being improved for the garden, with recent successes in tissue culture and hybridising greatly expanding their range, and they are as easy to grow and as beautiful as any exotics.

WILDFLOWER MEADOW GARDENS

For a no-fuss garden which is just that bit different, why not plant a wildflower meadow and then sit back and be surprised. A flowery meadow can be as big or as small as you like. It is just another form of traditional gardening; 'flowery medes' were features of medieval castle gardens, and flowering meadows only went out of fashion when lawnmowers were invented (curse the day!).

In awkward areas of the garden, a meadow is a good alternative. Difficult slopes and bumps are much more suited to an informal covering of flowers and grasses than a formal, labour-intensive lawn, and in an orchard, for example, a meadow garden is very practical. In windswept areas a ground-hugging meadow is best, perhaps using thyme and chamomile and erigeron species, all good on light soils, to create a living carpet.

Meadow plants need sun and you should choose species which can survive on natural rainfall. The idea is to create your own subtle ecosystem.

Probably the easiest way to provide a meadow is to simply stop mowing the lawn in spring and trust that some pretty grasses and wildflowers will emerge from amongst the ensuing long grass. Unfortunately, a good crop of vigorous weeds will more than likely result. One way to combat the weeds is to cover the existing grass with four or five layers of newspaper, and blanket it with a 10–15 centimetre depth of compost and soil. Seeds can be sown straight into the ground, but the best way to attain a meadow is to eliminate existing grass by spraying and then starting again. Of course this is a radical way and takes time and effort, but in the long run it will be labour-saving — no more lawnmowing. Once the ground is prepared, decide on a colour scheme, then select plants from the lists which follow.

Perennials for naturalising

Perennials for wildflower meadow gardens need to be hardy, and ones which increase readily by seed or division. In this situation you need perennials that spread and cause no trouble or require special nurturing.

CATANACHE	○
Cupid's dart	▲75 cm
Compositae	❖ Summer

The pretty, papery, blue flowers of *Catanache caerulea* bloom on wiry stems. You can cut and dry them and they are very hardy. Combine cupid's dart with yellow-flowering mountain tobacco, *Arnica montana*, and chicory, *Cichorium intybus*, for an eye-catching patch in the meadow garden.

CHRYSANTHEMUM	○
Feverfew; moon daisy	▲30–60 cm
Compositae	❖ Summer

Chrysanthemum parthenium (syn. *Tanacetum parthenium*) is a very hardy plant. Not

Trees are essential for large, rambling gardens.

Roses sit on the fence, and pink
'Parade' is a perfect foil for
white fantail doves, whilst
'Alchemist' and 'Crepuscule'
tumble over a brick arch.

long-lived and often grown as an annual, feverfew has bright aromatic foliage and small white daisy flowers with a yellow centre.

Often used as an edging plant, the moon daisy, *C. leucanthemum*, is ultra-hardy in coastal areas, and even in rough pasture.

CICHORIUM	○
Chicory	▲To 1 m
Compositae	❖ Summer–autumn

How about chicory, *Cichorium intybus*, for pretty sky-blue flowers? Often seen on roadsides, chicory has been in cultivation for thousands of years. The heavenly blue flowers close in the afternoon. Grow chicory with *Catanache caerulea*, to which it is closely related; cupid's dart is a darker blue. They both prefer lime in the soil, are grown from seed with ease and can be treated as annuals.

COREOPSIS	○
Compositae	▲60 cm
	❖ Summer–autumn

Coreopsis lanceolata is ultra-hardy and has become naturalised in many parts of Australia, where its shining yellow flowers make a grand display. *C. grandiflora* is similar, but bushier. Good for seaside places, too, and for cutting, coreopsis are as dazzling as a meadow of daffodils. 'Sunray' is a gold-medal winner. Semi-double, with butter-yellow flowers, this perennial is a precocious bloomer, and easily grown from seed, which should be sprinkled directly on to the ground where it is to flower.

OENOTHERA	○
Evening primrose	▲15 cm–1 m
Onagraceae	❖ Summer

Annuals, biennials and perennials, evening primroses, some of which bloom in the daytime, have strength and stamina. The perennial *Oenothera missouriensis* has lemon flowers, tolerates dry conditions, and opens in the evenings. *O. pallida* has fragrant white flowers and spreads well in a meadow garden. There are dozens of evening primrose varieties to choose from and all grow easily from seed, or by division.

VINCA	◑●
Periwinkle	▲Groundcover; to 10–15 cm
Apocynaceae	❖ Spring–summer

In the shady part of the garden trailing *Vinca major* and *V. minor* will do very well and introduce pretty blue and white flowers. They are semi-prostrate and have naturalised in many areas. Try to get *V. minor* 'Azurea Flore Pleno', which has double sky-blue flowers. Propagate by cuttings and division.

OTHER PERENNIALS SUITABLE FOR NATURALISING

Anthemis — chamomile	Origanum
Centranthus — valerian	Ornamental grasses
Digitalis — foxglove	Rudbeckia
Foeniculum — fennel	Solidago — golden rod
Knautia — field scabious	Thymus
Lupinus	

Bulbs for naturalising

Bulbs are right at home in the natural garden. Many bulbs are winter and spring flowering, just when meadow grasses and flowers have finished. You will want to cut these back in autumn, but from the end of April do not mow or cut this area, to allow the bulbs to come into their own.

ALLIUM	○
Ornamental onion	▲20 cm–1.5 m
Amaryllidaceae	❖ Summer–autumn

We are *not* talking the invasive onion flower here. The large, globular, blue-flowered *Allium caeruleum*, and *A. giganteum* with bright, round rosy flowerheads and stems a metre high, are the species to grow. *A. pulchellum* has graceful nodding flowers of violet. Persian onion, *A. christophii*, has unusual globular, net-like flowerheads, and *A. flavum* has flowers of shimmering yellow. Alliums need well-drained poor soil, as do most of the meadow bulbs. Divide large clumps after flowering.

AMARYLLIS	○
Belladonna lily	▲60 cm
Amaryllidaceae	❖ Late summer–autumn

Often seen in paddocks where old houses have been and gone, *Amaryllis belladonna* carries on steadily growing, flowering and multiplying. Bearing white, pink and deepest-pink trumpet flowers on stalwart stems, and blooming when many other subjects have finished, belladonnas look fresh, and smell good too in the meadow.

GALANTHUS	◐
Snowdrop	▲15–25 cm
Amaryllidaceae	❖ Winter–spring

In cool climates the snowdrop will naturalise in the meadow grasses. With white nodding bell flowers, the common snowdrop, *Galanthus nivalis*, multiplies quickly, and is at home in heavy soils. It has many variants, both single and double. Equally at home in woodland gardens, as long as they get sufficient moisture, snowdrops are very good for cutting.

IPHEION	◯◑
Amaryllidaceae	▲20 cm
	❖ Winter–spring

From Peru, *Ipheion uniflorum* (syn. *Tritelia uniflora*) has pale-blue starry blooms, which flower for up to 8 weeks, and grass-like leaves smelling slightly of onion. It is easy to grow in well-drained soil and soon multiplies. Ipheion can be grown in a meadow garden or on roadside verges in grass, and needs little attention.

NARCISSUS	◯◑
Daffodil; jonquil	▲20–45 cm
Amaryllidaceae	❖ Winter–spring

Daffodils and jonquils are perfect for naturalising in the meadow. The narcissus hybrids have complex, confusing parentage, but have larger, bolder flowers than their wild forebears. Double narcissus, trumpet daffodils, large cupped, small cupped, the split corona, tazetta and jonquils — all are hardy and all are beautiful, the very epitome of spring. In colours of yellow, gold, white, pink and apricot, narcissus blend exquisitely with meadow grasses and other bulbs. They are particularly in tune with linaria and forget-me-nots, often flowering at the same time, and very agreeable they look together.

WATSONIA	◯
Bugle lily	▲To 2 m
Iridaceae	❖ Early summer

Large, showy watsonias from South Africa will grow happily in the garden, in the meadow and on the roadside. Best in clumps, in warm climates watsonia species grow tall, with spikes of white, pink or salmon flowers. The glistening white-flowered varieties are outstanding. In some areas of Australia watsonias have naturalised.

OTHER BULBS SUITABLE FOR NATURALISING IN WILDFLOWER GARDENS

Camassia
Colchicum — autumn crocus
Crocosmia x *crocosmilflora*
Endymion (scilla) — bluebell
Ixia

Leucojum — snowflake
Sparaxis
Tritonia
Zantedeschia aethiopica — arum lily

Annuals for naturalising

Many annual flowers, grasses and herbs are eminently suitable for the wild meadow garden. Grow annuals appropriate to the natural character of the meadow — old-fashioned, simple flowers or grasses. Make successive sowings to prolong the display, and try lightly sowing some millet, wheat and barley amongst the flowers to give an effect.

AGROSTEMMA	○
Corn cockle	▲80 cm
Caryophyllaceae	❖ Summer

Corn cockles have rosy flowers atop slender stems. Sow them in clumps where they are to flower. The seeds are poisonous. They bloom for over 2 months and the winsome plump flowers in various colours are good for cutting. *Agrostemma githago* is outstanding.

AMMI	○
Queen Anne's lace	▲1–1.5 m
Umbelliferae	❖ Late spring

Many plants are known as 'Queen Anne's lace'; this is much prettier than the real thing. *Ammi majus* has large pure white florets as delicate as crochet work. Extremely easy to grow from seed, it can be dried for everlastings, and is excellent as a cut flower. Well worth growing anywhere in the garden, *A. majus* will complement any flower it is grown with. Other contenders for this title of 'Queen Anne's lace', such as *Daucus carota*, are also fine for meadow gardens.

ANETHUM	○
Dill	▲1 m
Umbelliferae	❖ Spring

Anethum graveolens is most decorative, with ferny, feathery foliage like a small fennel. Flowers are yellow on umbrella-shaped heads. You can use its leaves to flavour fish dishes, pickles and sauces. The seed can also be used for flavouring. Dill, like most herbs, favours a well-drained soil. Make successive sowings so you always have the aromatic young leaves on hand.

HORDEUM	○
Squirrel-tail grass	▲10–20 cm
Gramineae	❖ Mid-summer

Feathery, silvery, slender seedheads make *Hordeum jubatum* worthwhile in the meadow garden. A perennial grown as an annual, it is very easy to raise from seed.

Foxtail grass, *Setaria glauca*, has panicles of golden seedheads. Try a seed mixture of annual grasses.

LINARIA	◯◗
Bunny rabbit; toad flax	▲20–60 cm
Scrophulariaceae	❖ Winter

Flowering when many annuals have died down, toad flax, *Linaria maroccana*, is a valuable part of a meadow garden with its small snapdragon flowers in mauve and lemon or mixed violet, blue, red and pink shades. *L. reticulata* is taller, with dainty spurred flowers in similar colours. Sow in large quantities amongst meadow bulbs.

PAPAVER	◯
Poppy	▲50 cm
Papaveraceae	❖ Early–mid summer

Flanders, corn or field poppy, *Papaver rhoeas* (varieties include shirley poppies), have naturalised in parts of Europe. The brilliant scarlet flowers look wonderful in fields and meadow gardens. *P. commutatum* is similar, with crimson flowers and a black blotch. 'Flanders poppy' is a good variety — often listed as *P. rhoeas commutatum*. Grow poppies with cornflowers and wheat for the traditional look of English corn-fields. Sow all poppies in the ground where they are to flower.

OTHER ANNUALS SUITABLE FOR NATURALISING IN MEADOWS

Ammobium — winged everlasting
Centaurea — cornflower
Craspedia — billy buttons
Eschscholzia — California poppy
Helipterum — paper daisy
Myosotis — forget-me-not
Nigella — love-in-a-mist
Tropaeolum — nasturtium
Wheat, millet and barley

A BUSH GARDEN OF AUSTRALIAN PLANTS

Australia's flora offers gardeners some of the finest plants in the world, from huge eucalypts to minute groundcovers. Native Australian plants have a vibrancy of colour and form which makes them a natural choice. Most Australian plants are quick growing and evergreen; often they have fragrance in their leaves as well as their flowers. A bush garden filled with Australian species will reward its creator with early colour and a mature appearance within a short space of time.

There are other advantages, too. Many Australian plants produce copious quantities of nectar, so birds will frequent the garden regularly and a birdbath would be a welcome addition in summer. All year long, some plant or other will be in flower if you choose your species carefully. Use natural groundcovers in your bush, preferably bark. Do not attempt a lawn, but build meandering tracks, maybe gravelled or laid with bark chips, to lead visitors through the area. Plan your bush garden carefully, keeping in mind the ultimate height and shape of the trees and shrubs you select, and choosing your plants for colour, texture and foliage.

Australian trees and shrubs

A good stock of Australian trees and shrubs is readily available, and specialist seed packagers offer many varieties in their catalogues. Certain species are a must. The magnificent Proteaceae family is well represented; banksias, grevilleas, telopeas and dryandras are amongst the best. Acacias, eucalypts and callistemons are so well known they are often ignored as subjects for the home garden, but they are indispensable in problem areas. Eucalypts will also produce shelter and firewood if you have a large property.

ACACIA	○
Wattle	▲ 1–15 m
Leguminosae	❖ Winter–spring

Would a bush garden be complete without an acacia? Golden wattle, *Acacia pycnantha*, is Australia's national floral emblem. Acacias are a large genus, growing naturally thoughout Australia. At the seaside, in dry inland areas, bordering rainforests and in swamps, there will be an adaptable acacia. Not all are yellow flowered — they range from delicate cream through to brightest gold, and there is one pink-to-mauve species, *A. purpurepetala*. Cootamundra wattle, *A. baileyana*, with its ferny silver foliage and brilliant yellow winter flowers is always satisfying. Grow several of the same species together if you have room.

BAUERA	◑ ●
River rose	▲ 1.5 m
Baueraceae	❖ Spring

Cooler parts of the wild garden are ideal for *Bauera sessiliflora* and *B. rubioides*. Bauera have small leaves and open, six-petalled, palest-pink to deep-rose blooms. Mulch them well. You may have to water them in the driest weather as they are fond of moisture, but can't take wind. They are delightful shrubs to grow under tree ferns.

BUCKINGHAMIA	○
Ivory curl	▲ 2–10 m
Proteaceae	❖ Spring–winter

Proteaceae is a wondrous family, and well represented in Australia. *Buckinghamia celsissima* is a proud member — an attractive bushy shrub or small tree which is native to Queensland. Its curled, ivory flowers are similar to those of the grevillea, to which it is closely related. Ivory curl requires ample water and warmth, and is easily raised from seed. Mulch it well, and underplant with groundcovers such as *Hibbertia procumbens* and *Brachycome multifida*.

EPACRIS	◯◗
Australian native fuchsia	▲1–1.5 m
Epacridaceae	❖ Winter–summer

Epacris longiflora grows easily and thrives as long as the soil is well-drained and slightly acid. The flowers are long and tubular, cherry red, tipped white. Grow several together under eucalypts in dappled shade. Cut them back as they tend to get untidy, and propagate from cuttings. *E. pulchella* is smaller, with white and pink flowers, and is just as hardy.

EREMOPHILA	◯
Emu bush	▲1.5–2 m
Myoporaceae	❖ Spring–autumn

Birds will surely visit for the abundant nectar when emu bushes bloom. Many of the over 100 species will grow well in home gardens. Try *Eremophila glabra*, as it flowers nearly all year long, bearing unusual, bright scarlet blooms. Other species are yellow, green, white, pink and even purple, and all are drought resistant. Eremophilas like sunny places, but can be grown in a wide climate range. They are probably best sited at the edge of the bush garden.

HYMENOSPORUM	◯◗
Australian frangipani	▲6–7 m
Pittosporaceae	❖ Spring

This slender tree enjoys a warm, moist position and, if happy, will reward you with fragrant yellow blooms produced in abundance. The scent from the small bright flowers is intoxicating. Quick growing and precocious, *Hymenosporum flavum* has handsome leaves and does well in coastal districts, its natural habitat being rainforest areas in Queensland and NSW. A grove of these trees is most effective when underplanted with native shrubs and perennials. They tolerate light frosts.

MELALEUCA	◯◗
Myrtaceae	▲1–10 m
	❖ Spring–summer

Melaleucas, from shrubs to trees are found throughout Australia, some in swamps, others in arid areas. They bear bold, fluffy flowers in shades from white, green and lemon to orange and red. *Melaleuca fulgens* is a popular choice; its orange pom-

pom flowers are tipped with gold. M. *ericifolia*, with white flowers, is enchanting in the bush garden. There are 140 species of melaleuca, cousins to callistemons, and all encourage birds. Propagate from seed or cuttings.

TELOPEA	◯
Waratah	▲ 1–3 m
Proteaceae	❖ Spring

One of the best loved flowers of Australia, and NSW's floral emblem, the waratah, *Telopea speciosissima*, has ravishing flowers — large and dazzling scarlet blooms, brilliantly shaped. This prima donna is quite fussy, and unless given deep, well-drained soil, is apt to sulk and pine away of root rot. Waratahs are so special it is worthwhile persevering and spoiling them with optimum conditions. A white form is sometimes available, and is equally magnificent. Hybrids between the species — there are 4 of them — often produce tougher plants. Cut back after flowering.

OTHER AUSTRALIAN TREES AND SHRUBS

Agonis — willow myrtle
Backhousia citridora — lemon
    ironwood
Banksia
Boronia
Brachychiton acerifolius —
    Illawarra flame tree
Callistemon — bottlebrush
Correa — Australian fuchsia
Crowea — waxflower
Cyathea — tree fern
Dicksonia — tree fern

Dryandra
Eriostemon — waxflower
Eucalyptus
Grevillea
Hibbertia
Lambertia formosa — honey flower
Leptospermum — manuka; teatree
Pimelia
Prostanthera — mint bush
Schefflera actinophylla (syn.
    Brassaia actinophylla) —
    umbrella tree

Australian climbers

Climbers are a valuable part of the Australian bush, and many produce attractive berries much sought by birds. Shrubs and trees are hosts to climbers in the forest, and will provide this service in your bush garden. Choose climbers of a moderately vigorous nature, leaving the rampant varieties to clamber over old fallen logs and for banks. Climbers adorning trees and shrubs make good partnerships and help duplicate the lush, untrammelled atmosphere of the real bush.

BILLARDIERA	◯◖
Pottosporaceae	▲ 2–3 m
	❖ Spring–summer

Billardiera species are hardy climbers, well worth a place in the bush garden.

B. longiflora is of moderate vigour, and has long-lasting, creamy, tubular flowers followed by showy, shiny purple berries. The brilliant berries last right through the winter. In the wild garden *B. longiflora* is good for growing up a tree. There are more than 20 species to choose from, and all grow easily from seed.

KENNEDIA	○
Coral pea	▲2–4 m
Leguminosae	❖ Spring

Bright orange-red flowers cover the coral pea vine, *Kennedia coccinea*. It is a sturdy plant to smother an old shrub or stump or for trailing over a bank. Running postman, *K. prostrata*, hugs the ground and has scarlet flowers, whilst *K. nigricans* has surprising flowers of dark purple, almost black, with a smart dash of yellow. There are 15 species of kennedia, all tough, all liking well-drained soil and happily raised from seed.

SOLLYA	○
Bluebell creeper	▲2 m
Pittosporaceae	❖ Spring–summer

In the bush garden, *Sollya heterophylla*, the only species, grows well as it is easy-going about soil and will thrive in a wide range of conditions. The dainty bluebells, either light or dark blue, are followed by fleshy blue fruits. *S. heterophylla* can be trained as a bush, and is easily grown from seed or cuttings.

OTHER AUSTRALIAN CLIMBERS

Cissus — kangaroo vine
Hardenbergia — false sarsaparilla
Pandorea jasminoides — bower of
  beauty

P. pandorana — wonga wonga vine
Passiflora cinnabarina — red
  passionflower

Australian perennials

Australian native plants usually bear flowers in vibrant, primary colours. It is best to grow several of the same perennial species in drifts and clumps to re-create the effect of the natural bush; avoid 'cocktail' planting. Enhance the illusion with ferns — staghorns, elkhorns, bird's-nest ferns, giant tree ferns or minute maidenhairs. Kangaroo paws are Western Australia's floral emblem, and one of Australia's most well known perennials. You'll find them described in Chapter 2 on beds and borders (p. 32).

BLANDFORDIA	◯◗
Christmas bells	▲70 cm–1 m
Liliaceae	❖ Summer–autumn

In the bush garden *Blandfordia nobilis* is a decided asset, with its distinctive red and yellow bells on stiff stems — just right for the festive season. You need a drift of them for best effect. Christmas bells are good in containers, too, provided you give them generous draughts of water. In the garden they do well under trees. *B. grandiflora* needs more sun, but one from Tasmania, *B. punicea*, does well in shade. Blandfordias all require good drainage, and are easily raised from seed.

BRACHYCOME	◯◗
Compositae	▲30–40 cm
	❖ Spring–summer

Brachycome multifida, covered with lilac daisies amongst ferny foliage, is a rewarding plant. You need to grow several together. *B. rigidula* is best grown under shrubs with blue flowers. Other species are very good in the bush garden. The annual Swan River daisy, *B. iberidifolia*, is effective when grown en masse.

DENDROBIUM	◗●
Rock orchid	▲To 1 m
Orchidaceae	❖ Spring

Two forms of the ravishing rock orchid, *Dendrobium speciosum*, exist. Leaves of both are thick and strong. *D. speciosum* var. *hillii* is larger, with cream to yellow flowers. Do not attempt to grow your rock orchids in soil — nailed or tied on a tree or a rock is where they thrive. Rock orchids are right at home in the bush garden. The pink rock orchid, *D. kingianum*, is a hardy species and easy to grow. Dendrobiums are easier to cultivate than any other Australian orchid, and are the largest group.

DORYANTHES	◯
Gymea lily	▲To 4 m
Agavaceae	❖ Spring–summer

It is worth travelling a long way to see *Doryanthes excelsa* when it is in flower. The magnificent red flowerhead tops a spike up to 4 metres long which emerges from sword-like, metre-high leaves. This gymea lily will germinate readily from seed and takes about 7 years to flower. It grows naturally round Sydney in well-drained, warm soil. *D. palmeri* is similar in leaf but has a branched, arching flowerhead. It grows naturally in northern NSW and southern Queensland. Both varieties grow well in coastal conditions, but not if exposed to the elements.

SCAEVOLA	○
Fan flower	▲20 cm
Goodeniaceae	❖ Spring–autumn

This is a large genus of plants — shrubs, sub-shrubs and perennials. All have flowers in white or blue to purple, apart from a Queensland creeper with yellow flowers. A perennial groundcover, *Scaevola stricta*, the fan flower from Western Australia, has deep-blue blooms, likes a warm, well-drained spot, and will oblige by spreading for nearly a metre. It is easily propagated from cuttings and is excellent for a bush garden.

VIOLA	◑●
Australian native violet	▲7 cm
Violaceae	❖ Year round

A bush garden groundcover par excellence, *Viola hederacea* has enchanting flowers of blue-mauve and white. Its only fault is its lack of scent, but this is more than compensated for by its covering prowess and comeliness. To grow in the shade under trees or tree ferns, this violet is a great choice, and it will flourish right by the sea, as it does naturally in NSW as well as in the bush. For picking, the violets are long lasting and look most effective bunched or in a tussy mussy.

OTHER AUSTRALIAN PERENNIALS
Anigozanthos — kangaroo paw
Astelia alpina

Dampiera
Dianella
Lechenaultia

Australian annuals

Tourists flock to Australia, especially Western Australia, at wildflower time to see the incredible flora, unique to this isolated continent. The dazzling ephemerals which flower so lavishly will be at home in your bush garden until the trees and shrubs grow and shade the area. Most of the Australian native annuals like the wide open spaces. Many are also suitable for the wildflower garden.

CLIANTHUS	○
Sturt's desert pea	▲30 cm
Leguminosae	❖ Spring–summer

Sturt's desert pea, *Clianthus formosus*, is not easy to grow, but the flowers are so flamboyant and so evocative of Australia that it is worth persevering with. (It helps to have green fingers.) The national floral emblem of South Australia, this annual's natural habitat is sandy, arid soil over limestone. Limestone chips, placed some

15 cm deep in well-drained soil in a dry position, will make this clianthus feel at home. They resent being disturbed, and so it is best to sow them where they are to flower. Scarify the seed. You can make a mound in the natural garden and sow the seed on top. Watch out for slugs and snails.

CRASPEDIA	○
Billy buttons	▲20–50 cm
Compositae	❖ Summer

Billy buttons, *Craspedia globosa*, lighten the wild garden with their rounded yellow heads of flowers on stiff wiry stems amongst silver leaves. Excellent for cutting and drying, *C. globosa* is a perennial, best treated as an annual, and grows from seed with the greatest of ease. They are fun plants to grow in abundance, for they put up with dry conditions and are easy going. Great for the meadow garden, too.

HELICHRYSUM	○
Strawflower	▲To 1 m
Compositae	❖ Spring–autumn

Grown throughout the world, annual or perennial *Helichrysum bracteatum* are yellow and white in nature, but much work has been done on them in Europe to produce outstanding new strains of improved colour and size. Helichrysums are very hardy and most useful in the wild garden, either sown where they are to flower or transplanted. They need sun and good rich soil to be at their best. The perennial form is bushy, with grey, felted leaves and large, rather coarse, yellow flowers. It is ultrahardy and does not need as much attention as the annual variety. In the wild garden strawflowers will seed and multiply readily.

HELIPTERUM	○
Paper daisy	▲50 cm
Compositae	❖ Spring

Paper daisies, *Helipterum roseum* (syn. *Acrolinium roseum*) are a marvellous sight in Western Australia in spring, a major tourist attraction. An open, gritty soil suits them perfectly. Paper daisies should be sown with abandon where they are to flower if you want a show Western Australia would not spurn. The papery bracts are pink, white and rose, and last for years as dried flowers. Precocious plants, the flowers appear about 8 weeks after sowing, and bloom for the whole season, especially if you keep picking the open flowers. Paper daisies are fun for children to grow, as they mature so quickly and are a pleasure to pick and dry.

ISOTOMA ○◗

Lobeliaceae ▲30 cm

❖ Summer

Best treated as an annual, *Isotoma axillaris* is a delightful little plant with starry 5-petalled flowers. Several species are in cultivation, some having white flowers. Be careful handling the plants, for the sap stings and can cause a skin irritation. Isotomas grow readily from seed.

TRACHYMENE ○

Blue lace flower ▲60 cm

Umbelliferae ❖ Summer

Australia has many beautiful blue flowers. One of the best must be *Trachymene caerulea* which is noted for its soft, sky-blue, lacy blooms and ferny foliage. Grow them in drifts in well-drained soil. Trachymene species, both annual and perennial, are in shades of white, pink and blue. All are easy to grow from seed. Prick out the tops to encourage them to branch, and pick the flowers for the vase.

OTHER AUSTRALIAN ANNUALS

Ammobium — winged everlasting
Brachycome iberidifolia — Swan River daisy

Brunonia australis — blue pincushion
Hibiscus trionum
Waitzia acuminata — everlasting daisy

A BUSH GARDEN OF NEW ZEALAND PLANTS

Often not honoured in their own country, but warmly appreciated elsewhere, New Zealand's native plants are admirable anywhere in the garden. In awkward areas they shine, being hardy for the most part. If your site is hilly, windswept, dry, shady or swampy, there is a New Zealand native plant to suit. The choice is overwhelming.

Why not establish a grove of New Zealand trees and shrubs and underplant these with perennials and annuals? You will be creating a fascinating bush garden which will flourish year round, attract birds and help enrich your suburban environment. Visitors will be intrigued by it. Even in this small area of bush make room for a garden bench, maybe a bird feeder or a small pond. Traverse it with a path and make sure the area is well mulched. Once established, a bush garden of New Zealand species will virtually look after itself.

New Zealand trees and shrubs

The list of suitable New Zealand trees and shrubs for creating a bush garden is large, and your choice need be governed only by the site, soil and aspect. Do not select trees which grow too tall for the position. The opportunity New Zealand plants offer for unusual foliage effects should not be overlooked.

AGATHIS	◯◖
Kauri	▲4.5 m (in 15 years)
Araucariaceae	

King of the forest, the giant kauri, *Agathis australis*, is nevertheless suitable for an average property as it is so slow to mature, and does not spread itself, growing tall and slim. Kauris must have a soil which retains moisture. In years of drought they will die. The trunk of the young kauri (ricker) is most pleasing, with soft streaks of warm colours. Try growing a few together if possible, and mulch well whilst they are young. You can grow kauri from seed.

CORDYLINE	◯◖
Cabbage tree	▲4–10 m
Agavaceae	❖ Spring

The New Zealand cabbage tree, *Cordyline australis*, is much underrated by gardeners. It is palm-like in appearance, very hardy and grows in most situations. Grow several together, but not in a lawn as the leaves drop untidily. The large panicles of flowers are heavily scented and their glorious fragrance fills the air in spring. *C. indivisa* is the most handsome of the family, but will only grow in cool conditions, moist soil and away from the sea. *C. kaspar* does like the seaside, and is most presentable, with broad, dark heavy leaves. Dainty *C. pumilio* is grass-like, having no stems.

ENTELEA	◯◖
Whau	▲2.5–6 m
Tiliaceae	❖ Late spring

The large, heart-shaped leaves of this shrubby tree give the whau, *Entelea arborescens*, an exotic appearance. Hardy but frost tender, it is an asset to any type of garden. The cream flowers, borne in clusters, are followed by round, spiky seedheads. Whau is propagated from seed.

HEBE	◯◖
Scrophulariaceae	▲60 cm–2.5 m
	❖ Year round, but mostly spring

This large, diverse family has over 80 species and countless cultivars. Mostly hardy and easily grown, hebes are more appreciated in the Northern Hemisphere than they are in their native country. *Hebe hulkeana* is fragile looking, but is as hardy as others where there is little humidity. *H. speciosa* is indeed special, with purple flowers and glossy, dark-green leaves. It tackles salt winds without a qualm, and flowers for months on end. Low spreading *H. diosmifolia* can be planted in drifts and will produce white to mauve flowers. Cultivars abound. Clip back hebes and they will reward you with more flowers. If you grow only one New Zealand native groundcover in your bush garden, make it a hebe. Propagate from cuttings.

MACROPIPER	◐●
Kawakawa; pepper tree	▲2–3 m
Piperaceae	❖ Spring

If you have an awkward spot in your garden needing a quick-growing shrub, *Macropiper excelsum* could be the answer, for it is happy in difficult situations. The large, shiny leaves are often attacked by caterpillars in the summer, unfortunately. The bright orange drupes are edible, having a sweet, peppery flavour, they look and taste well in a savoury salad. *M. excelsum* is frost tender, but rather likes to be grown under trees where the frost will not touch it. The seeds germinate with ridiculous ease, and it is easily grown from cuttings.

OLEARIA	◐◗
Compositae	▲1–4 m
	❖ Spring

Olearia is a large genus of over 130 species, mainly from Australia and New Zealand. Species native to New Zealand are mostly white flowered. *Olearia arborescens* is showy, with attractive foliage, and the bush covers itself in white dainty flowers. *O. cheesemanii* is similar, and just as pleasing. A precocious shrub, it flowers when still young. Both species will grow in any well-drained soil. They are tolerant to wind and salt spray. *O. phlogopappa* is a most attractive Australian, with grey leaves and flowers of white, blue, pink or mauve. This one could be the prettiest olearia of the lot. Propagate from cuttings.

SOPHORA	◐◗
Kowhai	▲2.5–10 m
Leguminosae	❖ Spring

Kowhai are amongst the most spectacular of New Zealand's flowering trees and are almost a national emblem of that country. Hybrids exist between the two species, *Sophora tetraptera* and *S. microphylla*. Both species are hardy and not at all fussy about the soil they grow in. Birds are strongly attracted to the nectar of the kowhai's gorgeous yellow flowers. Kowhai are easily propagated from seed, which you need to presoak in hot water.

New Zealand climbers

New Zealand has some hardy native climbers. *Tecomanthe speciosa*, described in Chapter 9, is a notable example. Many have outstanding flowers and should not be overlooked for general use as well as in the bush garden.

CLEMATIS	◯◗
Bush clematis	▲To 12 m
Ranunculaceae	❖ Winter–spring

Clematis paniculata is New Zealand's well known white-flowered clematis. Happiest growing up a tree, *C. paniculata*, with its clean and shining flowers is the harbinger of spring in the bush. It blooms in late winter. Clematis need a cool run for their roots.

Other New Zealand clematis are also hardy and equally enchanting. Scented clematis, *C. parviflora*, has dark lime to lemon flowers which cover the plant. Green clematis, *C. hookeriana*, grows naturally over shrubs and small trees and is also sweetly scented. *C. petrei* is similar. All are easily raised from seed.

IPOMOEA	◯◗
Powhiwhi	▲6 m
Convolvulaceae	❖ Summer–autumn

Only suitable for warm, frost-free areas, *Ipomoea palmata* has large mauve flowers with a purple throat. It romps over shrubs and trees and can get out of hand unless you are careful, but being so easy going, it is well worthwhile in a difficult spot. Easily propagated from rooted cuttings, *I. palmata* has fresh, green, divided leaves.

Rata

METROSIDEROS	○
Climbing rata	▲To 18 m
Myrtaceae	❖ Spring

Metrosideros carminea has sparkling flowers of brilliant crimson and is one of the showiest of New Zealand natives. It attaches itself easily to walls and unsightly posts, and can also be trained as a shrub. (Nurseries stock both types.) M. *fulgens* is also worth growing. Grow your rata with kowhai and New Zealand flax, perhaps pink and red varieties.

TETRAPATHAEA	○◑
New Zealand passionflower	▲4 m
Passifloraceae	❖ Summer

With fragrant, greenish-white flowers, followed by orange berries in the autumn, *Tetrapathaea tetranda* is worth growing. It is hardy and will cling to a tree or any support you care to provide, or grow up a fence. As with many climbers, it rather likes a cool root run and its head in the sun. Propagate by cuttings.

New Zealand perennials

From groundcovers to bold grasses, New Zealand's flora contains a wealth of perennials. White-flowered plants are well represented, and many of these have handsome foliage. New Zealand flax must be one of the country's finest plant exports, and is a magnificent specimen for the garden in almost any situation. In the bush garden all these perennials are splendid for underplanting your groves of trees and shrubs.

ACAENA ○◗
Bidibidi	▲Groundcover
Rosaceae	❖ Summer

Pretty little things, bidibidi can be grown as a groundcover in awkward areas, on a slope or in gravelly poor soil. A warning: do not plant it where you walk, for the burrs stick like glue. *Acaena microphylla* has fern-like foliage and will carpet an area quickly. It has bronze leaves and round lime and wine burr-like blooms. Be careful with this plant, for it can become invasive.

ASTELIA ○◗
Liliaceae	▲1 m
	❖ Spring

Dramatic *Astelia chathamica* has glistening, silver, sword-like foliage. Easy-to-grow astelias are happy in many diverse situations. Under trees and tree ferns they do well, and they can be propagated easily by division. In nature some species grow in the forks of trees.

CHIONOCHLOA ○
Gramineae	▲1 m
	❖ Summer

Chionochloa flavicans is a hardy grass which has delightful fluffy seedheads, very good for dried arrangements. Easily grown in an open situation or on a bank, *C. flavicans* is worth a place in the garden. It can be propagated from seed or by division. *C. rubra* is another species worthy of garden space.

GERANIUM ○
Geraniaceae	▲25 cm
	❖ Spring

Geranium traversii has bright pink flowers, surprising in a New Zealand native. The grey foliage sets them off perfectly. It is very hardy but does need a sunny position, so is well suited for a rock garden or exposed bank, and is easily rooted from cuttings taken in spring. *G. traversii* grows well with *Chionochloa flavicans*.

PACHYSTEGIA ○
Marlborough rock daisy	▲To 90 cm
Compositae	❖ Summer

Pachystegia insignis positively revels in hostile conditions, and as long as you have a well-drained, sunny position, this rock daisy will flourish. The daisies are a silky grey in bud, opening to a clear white. Several together are good for impact, and you can grow them quite happily in containers.

SCLERANTHUS	◯◗
Mossy scabweed	▲Groundcover
Caryophyllaceae	

If you have a site causing despair, poor, stony and barren, try the ground-hugging *Scleranthus biflorus*, a brilliant green, mossy-looking plant. It grows naturally in dry riverbeds. It would be ideal, too, in a Japanese-type garden, for its trim, tiny hillocks have an oriental look. You could also grow it with *Raoulia australis*, another hardy groundcover.

OTHER NEW ZEALAND PERENNIALS

Arthropodium — renga renga; rock lily
Bulbinella — Maori onion
Carex petrei
Cotula
Dianella — blueberry; turutu
Ferns
Gunnera propens

Libertia
Linum — New Zealand linen flax
Mazus
Myosotidium — Chatham Island forget-me-not
Phormium — New Zealand flax
Pratia angulata
Xeronema — Poor Knights lily

INDEX

Page numbers in bold refer to plant descriptions.

Creeping fig, **14**, 20, 53, 104, 116, 136
Crepe myrtle, **26**, 73
Crinum, **34**, 37, 118
Crocus, 35, 36, 37, 38
Crocosmia, 147
Crotalaria, 102
Croton, **95**
Crowea, 27, 152
Crucifix orchid, **81**
Ctenanthe, 96
Cup of gold, 15, **115**
Cupid's dart, **144**
Cupressus, 55, **70**, 114
Currant, flowering, 27
Cyathea, 123, **133**, 152, 160
Cycas, 134
Cyclamen, **139**
Cymbalaria, **66**
Cynara, **33**
Cynoglossum, 41
Cyperus, **124**
Cypress, 55, **70**, 114
Cytisus, 13, 19, 25, 28, 102

D

Dacrydium, 73, **133**, 160
Daffodil, 38, 84, **147**
Dahlia, 31, 42
Dampiera, 155
Daphne, 19, 27, **59**, 134
Day lily, 31, **32**, 117, 138
Delphinium, **30**
Dendrobium, **154**
Deutzia, 27, 59
Dianella, 155, 163
Dianthus, 29, 34, 42, **59**, 62, 64
Diascia, 31, 82
Dicentra, 138
Dicksonia, 134, 152, 160
Dieffenbachia, 96
Dierama, **36**
Digitalis, 40, **140**, 146
Dill, **148**
Dimorpotheca, **108**, 119
Dionaea, 97
Diosma, 25, 27
Dog's tooth violet, **139**
Dogwood, 73, 134
Doryanthes, **154**
Dracaena, **90**
Drumstick primula, **125**
Dryandra, 102, 152
Dumb cane, 96

Dusty miller, 34, 119
Dutch iris, **35**

E

Eccremocarpus, 80
Echevaria, 67, 96, 105
Echinops, 30, 34
Echium, 102, **108**, **117**
Edgeworthia, 28
Elaeocarpus, 160
Elephant's ear, 96, 138
Elodia, **129**
Emu bush, **151**
English daisy, 42, 85
English iris, **35**
Endymion, 36, 140, 147
Enkianthus, 134
Entelea, 114, **158**
Epacris, 134, **151**
Epidendrum, **81**
Epimedium, **60**
Episcia, 97
Eremophila, **151**
Erica, **19**, 25, 59, 102
Erigeron, 17, 21, 61, **66**, 82
Eriostemon, 13, 134, 152
Eryngium, **30**, 105, 117
Erythronium, **139**
Escallonia, 48
Eschscholzia, **17**, 43, 109, 119, 149
Eucalyptus, 73, **101**, 152
Eucharis, **97**
Eucomis, 35
Euphorbia, 27, 33, 40, 51, **90**, 102, 105
Euryops, **12**, 102
Evening primrose, **145**
Everlasting daisy, 157

F

Fagus, 48
Fairy primula, 40, 42, 62, 85, 141
False cypress, **54**, 73
False sarsaparilla, 15, 20, **103**, 116, 136, 153
Fan flower, 17, 117, **155**
Fatshedera, 133
Fatsia, 51, **133**
Feijoa, **47**, 114
Felicia, 13, 26, 61, 82, **104**, 117
Fennel, 146
Fern, **95**, 96, 127, 163
Fescue, blue, **33**
Festuca, **33**

Mock orange, 25, 134
Monkey flower, 127, 141
Monkshood, 138
Monstera, 96, 136
Moon daisy, **144**
Moonflower, **78**, 93
Moraea, 36
Morning glory, 80, **94**
Moss phlox, **64**
Mossy scabweed, **163**
Mother-in-law's tongue, 96
Mountain tobacco, **144**
Mouse plant, 140
Muscari, **35**, 84, 140
Myoporum, 102, 114, 160
Myosotidium, 117, **138**, 163
Myosotis, 41, **141**, 149
Myrtle, 48
Myrtus, 48

N

Nandina, **50**
Narcissus, 35, 38, 84, 140, **147**
Nasturtium, **17**, 43, 85, 109, 119, 149
Nelumbo, **128**
Nemesia, 41, **85**
Nemophila, **40**, 62, 141
Nepeta, **105**
Nephrolepis, **96**
Nerine, 35, 37, 84, **107**
Nerium, 25, 48, 102
Never-never plant, 96
New Zealand Christmas tree, **113**
New Zealand flax, 17, 67, **117**, 127, 163
New Zealand glory pea, **18**, 152
New Zealand hibiscus, 43, **119**
New Zealand linen flax, 163
New Zealand native broom, 160
New Zealand passionflower, **161**
Ngaio, 102, 114, 160
Nicotiana, 40, 42
Nierembergia, 61, 64
Nigella, **40**, 141, 149
Nikau palm, 134, 160
Nopalxochia, 97
Norfolk Island hibiscus, 102, **113**
Norfolk pine, **112**
Nuphar, 129
Nymphaea, 82, **128**
Nymphoides, 129

O

Ocimum, **85**
Oenothera, **145**
Olea, **101**
Oleander, 25, 48, 102
Olearia, 26, 114, **159**
Olive, **101**
Omphalodes, 30, 40
Onion, ornamental, 36, 37, 107, 118, **146**
Opium poppy, 40, 42
Orchid cactus, 97
Origanum, **81**, 146
Ornithogalum, 35
Orontium, 129
Osmunda, 127
Osteospermum, **16**, 21, 117
Oxygenators **129**
Oxypetalum, 26, **59**

P

Pachystegia, **162**
Paeonia, 25, 27, 29, **31**, 33
Painted daisy, 31
Palm, **70**, 78, **90**, 102, 114
Pampas grass, 117
Pandorea, **14**, **52**, 80, 87, 153
Pansy, 41, **42**
Papaver, 40, 42, 43, **149**
Paper daisy, 109, 149, **156**
Papyrus, **124**
Parapara, 92
Parlour palm, **90**
Parochetus, 127, 138
Parrot flower, 97
Parthenocissus, **52**
Pasque flower, 30
Passiflora, 53, 80, **86**, 153
Passionflower, 53, 80, **86**, 153, **161**
Pate, 134, 160
Peach, ornamental, **72**
Peacock plant, 96
Pelargonium, 17, **20**, 53, 67, **82**, 104
Penstemon, 31
Pentas, 78
Peony, 25, 27, 29, **31**, 33
Peperomia, 96
Pepper tree, 102, **159**
Pereskia, 93
Periwinkle, 67, **145**
Pernettya, **122**, 134
Peruvian lily, **32**
Petrea, 116

ACKNOWLEDGEMENTS

I wish to thank the following for all their generous help and encouragement —
Julian Matthews, without whom this book would not have been written;
Christine Moffat, patient and supportive editor at Penguin Books; Joy Browne,
book editor and dear friend and mentor; my husband, whose optimism
sustained me.

The publisher would like to thank those people whose gardens are featured in this book.
The following list notes the details of location for each photograph.

Photographs by Julian Matthews:

i (top) Hokonui Alpines, Gore; **i (bottom)** Lucy and Les Taylor, New Plymouth; **ii (top left)** Pauline
Lepper, New Plymouth; **ii (right)** Omahanui: Toni and Ron Sylvester, Auckland; **ii (bottom)**
Havelock North; **iii (top left)** Mangarara: Heather and John Dean, Nuhaka; **iii (left)** Pauline Lepper,
New Plymouth; **iii (bottom)** The Ridges Garden, Marton; **iv (bottom)** Hokonui Alpines, Gore;
iv (right) Shirley Greenhill, Stratford; **v (bottom)** Bob Gibbs, Waikanae; **v (top)** Gwyn Masters,
Stratford: **vi (right)** Judy and Arthur Bills, Waikanae; **vi (bottom)** Noel Scotting, Howick,
Auckland; **viii** Ormonds' Garden and Nursery, Havelock North; **ix (top)** Roadside, Waikanae;
x (top right) Judy and Arthur Bills, Waikanae; **x (right)** Shirley Greenhill, Stratford: **x (bottom)**
Barbara Toogood, Havelock North; **xi (top right)** Crosshills: Elizabeth Robertson, Otorohanga;
xi (left) Trelinnoe Scenic Gardens, Te Pohue; **xi (bottom)** Maple Glen: Muriel Davison, Wyndham,
Southland; **xii (right)** Blue Cliffs, South Canterbury; **xiii (top right)** Ohinetahi: Governors Bay,
Canterbury; **xiv (right)** Tupare, New Plymouth; **xiv (bottom)** Titoki Point: Gordon Collier,
Taihape; **xv (top)** Ohinetahi: Governors Bay, Canterbury; **xv (bottom)** Maple Glen: Muriel
Davison, Wyndham, Southland; **xvi (top left)** Pauline Lepper, New Plymouth; **xvi (right)**
Omahanui: Toni and Ron Sylvester, Auckland; **xvi (bottom)** Lyn Atkinson, Sumner, Christchurch.

Photographs by Gil Hanly:

vii (top) Mrs G. Hill, Auckland; **vii (bottom)** Frances Wilson, Parnell, Auckland; **ix (bottom)** Dinah
Firth, Herne Bay, Auckland; **xii (bottom)** Barry Lett, Mt Albert, Auckland; **xiii (bottom)** Harley
Hansen, Parnell, Auckland; **xiii (top left)** Joan Innes, Christchurch; **front cover:** Dinah Firth,
Herne Bay, Auckland.